Rick Steves®

SNAPSHOT

Northern Ireland

T0002316

CONTENTS

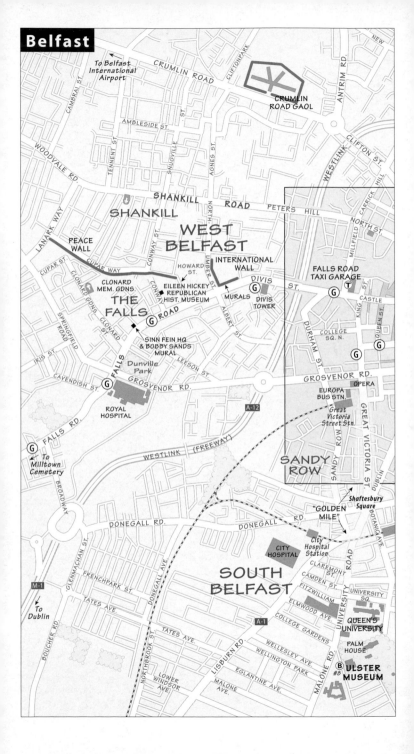

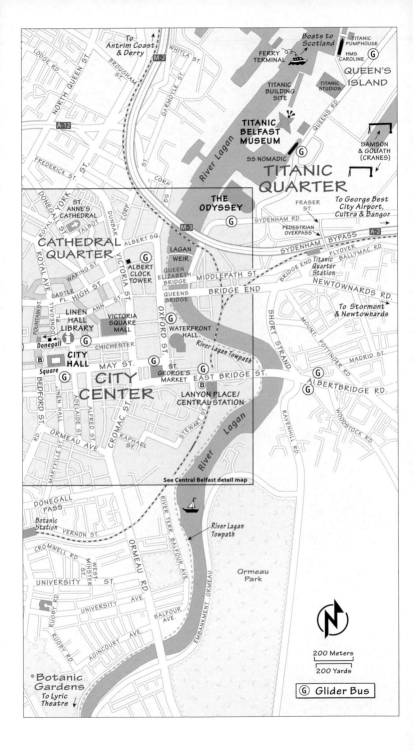

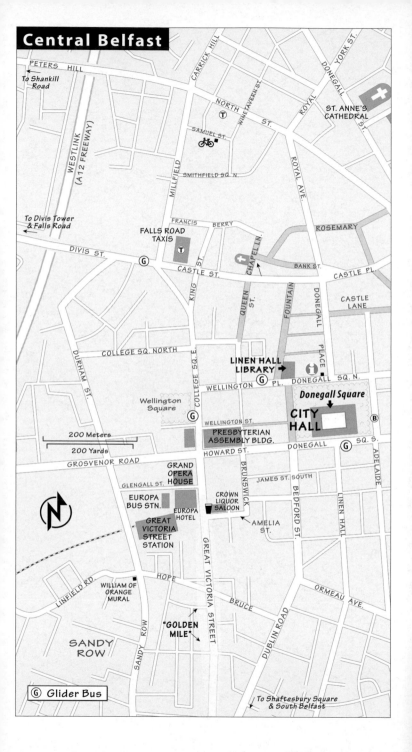

Central Belfast

PETERS HILL
To Shankill Road

WESTLINK (A12 FREEWAY)

CARRICK HILL

WHITETAVERN ST.

DONEGALL ST.

YORK ST.

ROYAL ST.

ST. ANNE'S CATHEDRAL

NORTH ST.

SAMUEL ST.

MILLFIELD

SMITHFIELD SQ. N.

ROYAL AVE.

FRANCIS ST.

BERRY ST.

ROSEMARY

To Divis Tower & Falls Road

FALLS ROAD TAXIS

CHAPEL LN.

BANK ST.

DIVIS ST.

CASTLE ST.

CASTLE PL.

KING ST.

QUEEN ST.

FOUNTAIN ST.

DONEGALL PLACE

CASTLE LANE

DURHAM ST.

COLLEGE SQ. NORTH

COLLEGE SQ. E.

LINEN HALL LIBRARY

WELLINGTON PL.

DONEGALL SQ. N.

Wellington Square

WELLINGTON ST.

Donegall Square

CITY HALL

DONEGALL SQ. S.

B

ADELAIDE

200 Meters

200 Yards

GROSVENOR ROAD

PRESBYTERIAN ASSEMBLY BLDG.

HOWARD ST.

BRUNSWICK

JAMES ST. SOUTH

BEDFORD ST.

LINEN HALL ST.

N

GLENGALL ST.

GRAND OPERA HOUSE

CROWN LIQUOR SALOON

EUROPA BUS STN.

EUROPA HOTEL

AMELIA ST.

GREAT VICTORIA STREET STATION

LINFIELD RD.

WILLIAM OF ORANGE MURAL

HOPE ST.

SANDY ROW

SANDY ROW

GREAT VICTORIA STREET

BRUCE ST.

ORMEAU AVE.

"GOLDEN MILE"

DUBLIN ROAD

To Shaftesbury Square & South Belfast

G Glider Bus

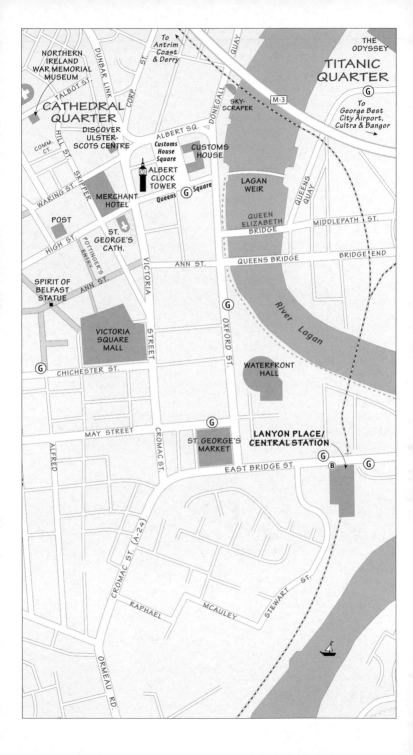

INTRODUCTION

This Snapshot guide, excerpted from my guidebook *Rick Steves Ireland*, introduces you to Northern Ireland—an underrated and often overlooked part of the Emerald Isle that surprises visitors with its friendliness. I've included a lively mix of cities (Belfast and Derry), smaller towns (Portrush and Bangor), and plenty of lazy rural sights. History is palpable atop the brooding walls of Derry and in the remote and traditional countryside. And, while it's perfectly safe for a visit, Northern Ireland gives you a feel for Ireland's 20th-century "Troubles" as nowhere else—especially the provocative political murals in Derry's Bogside neighborhood, and on Belfast's Falls Road and Shankill Road. You'll also find enjoyable escapes: From the breezy seaside resort of Portrush, you can visit the scenic Antrim Coast—which boasts the unique staggered-columns geology of the Giant's Causeway, the spectacularly set Dunluce Castle, and a chance to sample whiskey at Old Bushmills Distillery.

To help you have the best trip possible, I've included the following topics in this book:

• **Planning Your Time,** with advice on how to make the most of your limited time

• **Orientation,** including tourist information (abbreviated as TI), tips on public transportation, local tour options, and helpful hints

• **Sights,** with ratings and strategies for meaningful and efficient visits

• **Sleeping** and **Eating,** with good-value recommendations in every price range

• **Connections,** with tips on trains, buses, and driving

Practicalities, near the end of this book, has information on money, staying connected, hotel reservations, transportation, and other helpful hints.

To travel smartly, read this little book in its entirety before you go. It's my hope that this guide will make your trip more meaningful and rewarding. Traveling like a temporary local, you'll get the absolute most out of every mile, minute, and dollar.

Happy travels!

Rick Steves

Northern Ireland

NORTHERN IRELAND

 Northern Ireland is a different country than the Republic—both politically (it's part of the United Kingdom) and culturally (a combination of Irish, Scottish, and English influences). Occupying the northern one-sixth of the island of Ireland, it's only about 12 miles from Scotland at the narrowest point of the North Channel, and bordered on the south and west by the Republic.

When you leave the Republic of Ireland and enter Northern Ireland, you are crossing an international border. For years, the border has been almost invisible, without passport checks, though Brexit, the UK's withdrawal from the EU, could potentially change the way the border is handled in the future (see "The Brexit Effect" sidebar, later).

You won't use euros here; Northern Ireland issues its own Ulster pound, which, like the Scottish pound, is interchangeable with the English pound (€1=about £0.85; £1=about $1.30). Price differences create a lively daily shopping trade for those living near the border. Some establishments near the border may take euros, but at a lousy exchange rate. Keep any euros for your return to the Republic, and get pounds from an ATM inside Northern Ireland instead. And if you're heading to Britain next, it's best to change your Ulster pounds into English ones (free at any bank in Northern Ireland, England, Wales, or Scotland).

But some differences between Northern Ireland and the Republic are disappearing: Following the Republic's lead, Northern Ireland legalized same-sex marriage and decriminalized abortion in 2019 (also bringing its legislation more in line with rest of the United Kingdom).

Northern Ireland has emerged from the dark shadow of the decades-long political strife and violence known as the Troubles. While not as popular among tourists as its neighbor to the south, Northern Ireland offers plenty to see and do...and learn.

It's important for visitors to Northern Ireland to understand the ways in which its population is segregated along political, religious, and cultural lines. Roughly speaking, the eastern seaboard is more Unionist, Protestant, and of English-Scottish heritage, while

NORTHERN IRELAND

Northern Ireland Almanac

Official Name: Northern Ireland (pronounced "Norn Iron" by locals). Some call it Ulster (although historically that term included three counties that today lie on the Republic's side of the border), while others label it the Six Counties.

Size: 5,400 square miles (about the size of Connecticut), constituting a sixth of the island. With 1.8 million people, it's the smallest of the four United Kingdom countries (the others are England, Wales, and Scotland).

Geography: Northern Ireland is shaped roughly like a doughnut, with the UK's largest lake in the middle (Lough Neagh, 150 square miles and a prime eel fishery). Gently rolling hills of green grass rise to the 2,800-foot Slieve Donard. The weather is temperate, cloudy, moist, windy, and hard to predict.

Latitude and Longitude: 54°N and 5°W (as far north as parts of the Alaskan panhandle).

Biggest Cities: Belfast, the capital, has 300,000 residents. Half a million people—nearly one in three Northern Irish—inhabit the greater Belfast area. Derry (called Londonderry by Unionists) has 110,000 people.

Economy: Northern Ireland's economy is more closely tied to the UK than to the Republic of Ireland, and is subsidized by the UK. Traditional agriculture (potatoes and grain) is fading fast, but Northern Ireland remains a major producer of sheep, cows, and grass seed. Modern software and communications companies are replacing traditional manufacturing. Once-proud shipyards are rusty relics, and the linen industry is now threadbare.

Government: Northern Ireland is not a self-governing nation, but is part of the UK, ruled from London by Queen Elizabeth II and Prime Minister Boris Johnson, and represented by 18 elected Members of Parliament. For 50 years (1922-1972), Northern Ireland was granted a great deal of autonomy and self-governance, known as "Home Rule." Today some decisions are delegated to a National Assembly (90-seat Parliament), but political logjams often render it ineffective.

Flag: The official flag of Northern Ireland is the Union flag of the UK. But you'll also see the green, white, and orange Irish tricolor (waved by Nationalists) and the Northern Irish flag (white with a red cross and a red hand  at its center), which is used by Unionists (see "The Red Hand of Ulster" sidebar on page 91).

the south and west (bordering the Republic of Ireland) are Nationalist, Catholic, and of indigenous Irish descent. Cities are often clearly divided between neighborhoods of one group or the other. Early in life, locals learn to identify the highly symbolic (and highly charged) colors, jewelry, sports jerseys, music, names, accents, and vocabulary that distinguish the cultural groups.

The roots of Protestant and Catholic differences date back to the time when Ireland was a colony of Great Britain. Four hundred years ago, Protestant settlers from England and Scotland were strategically "planted" in Catholic Ireland to help assimilate the island into the British economy. In 1620, the dominant English powerbase in London felt entitled to call both islands—Ireland as well as Britain—the "British Isles" on maps (a geographic label that irritates Irish Nationalists to this day). These Protestant settlers established their own cultural toehold on the island, laying claim to the most fertile land. Might made right, and God was on their side. Meanwhile, the underdog Catholic Irish held strong to their Gaelic culture on their ever-diminishing, boggy, rocky farms.

Over the last century, the conflict between these two groups has not been solely about faith. Heated debates today are usually about politics: Will Northern Ireland stay part of the United Kingdom (Unionists), or become part of the Republic of Ireland (Nationalists)?

By the beginning of the 20th century, the sparse Protestant population could no longer control the entire island. When Ireland won its independence in 1921 (after a bloody guerrilla war against British rule), 26 of the island's 32 counties became the Irish Free State, ruled from Dublin with dominion status in the British Commonwealth—similar to Canada's level of sovereignty. In 1949, these 26 counties left the Commonwealth altogether and became the Republic of Ireland, severing all political ties with Britain. Meanwhile, the six remaining northeastern counties—the only ones with a Protestant majority who considered themselves British—chose not to join the Irish Free State and remained part of the UK.

But within these six counties—now joined as the political entity called Northern Ireland—was a large, disaffected Irish (mostly Catholic) minority who felt marginalized by the drawing of the new international border. This sentiment was represented by the Irish Republican Army (IRA), who wanted all 32 of Ireland's counties to be united in one Irish nation—their political goals were "Nationalist." Their political opponents were the "Unionists"—Protestant British eager to defend the union with Britain, who were primarily led by two groups: the long-established Orange Order, and the military muscle of the newly mobilized Ulster Volunteer Force (UVF).

In World War II, the Republic stayed neutral while Northern Ireland enthusiastically supported the Allied cause—winning a spot close to London's heart. Derry (a.k.a. Londonderry) became an essential Allied convoy port, while Belfast lost more than 900 civilians during four Luftwaffe bombing raids in 1941. After the war, the split between North and South seemed permanent, and Britain invested heavily in Northern Ireland to bring it solidly into the UK fold.

In the Republic of Ireland, where the population was 94 percent Catholic and only 6 percent Protestant, there was a clearly dominant majority. But in Northern Ireland, Catholics were a sizable 35 percent of the population—enough to demand attention when they exposed anti-Catholic discrimination on the part of the Protestant government. It was this discrimination that led to the Troubles, the conflict that filled headlines from the late 1960s to the late 1990s.

Partly inspired by Martin Luther King, Jr. and the civil rights movement in America, in the 1960s the Catholic minority in Northern Ireland began a nonviolent struggle to end discrimination, advocating for better jobs and housing. Extremists polarized issues, and once-peaceful demonstrations became violent.

Unionists were afraid that if the island became one nation, the relatively poor Republic of Ireland would drag down the comparatively affluent North. They also feared losing political power to a Catholic majority. As the two sides clashed in 1969, the British Army entered the fray. Their role, initially a peacekeeping one, gradually evolved into acting as muscle for the Unionist government. In 1972, more than 500 people died as combatants moved from petrol bombs to guns, and a new, more violent IRA emerged. In the 30-year (1968-1998) chapter of the struggle for an independent and united Ireland, more than 3,000 people died.

In the 1990s—with the UK (and Ireland's) membership in the EU, the growth of its economy, and the weakening of the Catholic Church's authority—the Republic of Ireland's influence became less threatening to the Unionists. Optimists hailed the signing of a breakthrough peace plan in 1998, called the "Good Friday Agreement" by Nationalists, or the "Belfast Agreement" by Unionists. This led to the release of political prisoners on both sides in 2000—a highly emotional event.

British Army surveillance towers in Northern Ireland's cities were dismantled in 2006, and the army formally ended its 38-year-long Operation Banner campaign in 2007. In 2010, the peace process was jolted forward by a surprisingly forthright apology offered by then-British Prime Minister David Cameron. The apology was prompted by the Saville Report—the results of an investigation conducted by the UK government as part of the Good Friday Agreement. It found that the 1972 shootings of Nationalist civil-rights marchers—known as Bloody Sunday—by British soldiers was "unjustified" and the victims innocent (vindication for the victims' families, who had fought since 1972 to clear their loved ones' names).

Major hurdles to a lasting peace persist. Occasionally backward-thinking extremists ape the brutality of their grandparents' generation. And with the UK leaving the European Union, many worry that tensions between the Republic and Northern Ireland will flare up. But the downtown checkpoints are long gone, replaced by a forest of construction cranes, especially in rejuvenated Belfast.

When locals spot you with a map and a lost look on your face, they're likely to ask, "Wot yer lookin fer?" in their distinctive Northern accent. They're not suspicious of you, but trying to help you find your way. They may even "giggle" (Google) it for you. You're safer in Belfast than in many UK cities—and far safer, statistically, than in most major US cities. Just don't seek out spit-and-sawdust pubs in working-class neighborhoods and spew simplistic opinions about sensitive local topics. Tourists notice lingering tension mainly during the "marching season" (Easter-Aug), culminat-

Northern Ireland Terminology

You may hear Northern Ireland referred to as **Ulster**—the traditional name of Ireland's ancient northernmost province. When the Republic of Ireland became independent in 1922, six of the nine counties of Ulster elected to form Northern Ireland, while three counties joined the Republic.

The mostly Protestant **Unionist** majority—and the more hardline, working-class **Loyalists**—want to remain part of the UK. The **Ulster Unionist Party** (UUP) is the political party representing moderate Unionist views (Nobel Peace Prize co-winner David Trimble led the UUP from 1995 to 2005). The **Democratic Unionist Party** (DUP) takes a harder stance in defense of Unionism. The **Ulster Volunteer Force** (UVF), the **Ulster Freedom Fighters** (UFF), and the **Ulster Defense Association** (UDA) are Loyalist paramilitary organizations: All three are labeled "proscribed groups" by the UK's 2000 Terrorism Act.

The mostly Catholic **Nationalist** minority—and the more hardline, working-class **Republicans**—want a united and independent Ireland ruled by Dublin. The **Social Democratic Labor Party** (SDLP), founded by Nobel Peace Prize co-winner John Hume, is the moderate political party representing Nationalist views. **Sinn Féin** takes a harder stance in defense of Nationalism. The **Irish Republican Army** (IRA) is the now-disarmed Nationalist paramilitary organization historically linked with Sinn Féin. The **Alliance Party** wants to bridge the gap between Unionists and Nationalists.

The long-simmering struggle to settle Northern Ireland's national identity precipitated the **Troubles,** the violent, 30-year conflict (1968-1998) between Unionist and Nationalist factions. To gain more insight into the complexity of the Troubles, the 90-minute documentary *Voices from the Grave* provides an excellent overview (easy to find on YouTube). Also check out the University of Ulster's informative and evenhanded Conflict Archive at https://cain.ulster.ac.uk.

Northern Ireland Politics

NATIONALISTS
(MOSTLY CATHOLICS)
"Feel Irish""

UNIONISTS
(MOSTLY PROTESTANTS)
"Feel British"

SINN FEIN

ALLIANCE

DUP

SDLP
*John Hume
(retired)*

UUP
*David Trimble
(retired)*

MODERATES

REPUBLICANS

LOYALISTS

GREEN

ORANGE

Not to scale &
not all opinions shown

NORTHERN IRELAND

The Brexit Effect

Brexit—the UK's decision to leave the European Union—has only stoked longstanding tensions within the UK's member nations.

The people of the United Kingdom narrowly approved the referendum—but in Northern Ireland, as in Scotland, a majority of people voted to remain. Scotland is flirting with independence: Separating from the UK would allow it to stay in the EU. The Republic of Ireland (an EU member) fills more than 80 percent of the island of Ireland; a growing minority in Northern Ireland would like to see the island come together as a single Irish nation—inside the EU.

Which direction will the north lean? Special status within the UK? Reunification with the Republic?

The Good Friday Agreement that ended the Troubles assumed there'd be open borders between Northern Ireland and the Republic. But with the UK leaving the EU, one of the largest questions is what form the new border will take. Few want a "hard border," with trade tariffs and border controls between EU and UK zones. For example, the Northern Ireland border city of Derry has a struggling economy that relies on easy access to rural County Donegal, next door in the Republic. Making that market harder to reach would cause further hardship to a vulnerable community.

Beyond the economics, a hard border could add fuel to "them and us" perceptions, rekindling tension between dormant Republican and Loyalist extremists. No one wants to go back to the days when the border between Northern Ireland and the Republic was a closely patrolled line in a war zone.

Some Northern Irelanders are hedging their bets: Anyone born in Northern Ireland is eligible for a British passport, an Irish one, or both. Traditionally, Nationalist Catholics chose an Irish one and Unionist Protestants went for a British one. But with Brexit, many staunchly loyal Unionists quietly applied for Irish passports to keep their options open.

Stay tuned to see how the swirling currents of Brexit, the Scottish independence movement, and the Irish reunification dream will affect this unique corner of the world...perched precariously between diverging cultural and economic powers: Ireland, Scotland, and England.

ing on July 12—"the Twelfth"—when proud Protestant Unionist Orangemen march to celebrate their Britishness (often through staunchly Nationalist Catholic neighborhoods—it's still good advice to lie low if you stumble onto any big Orange parades).

One of Northern Ireland's most valuable assets is its industrious people (the "Protestant work ethic"). When they emigrated to the US, they became known as the Scots-Irish and played a crucial role in our nation's founding. They were signers of our Declaration of Independence, a dozen of our presidents (think tough-as-nails "Old Hickory" Andrew Jackson as a classic example), and the ancestors of Davy Crockett and Mark Twain.

Northern Irish workers have a proclivity for making things that go. They've produced far-reaching inventions like Dunlop's first inflatable tire. The Shorts aircraft factory (in Belfast) built the Wright Brothers' first aircraft for commercial sale and the world's first vertical takeoff jet. The *Titanic* was the only flop of Northern Ireland's otherwise successful shipbuilding industry. The once-futuristic DeLorean sports car was made in Belfast.

Notable people from Northern Ireland include musicians Van Morrison and James Galway, and actors Liam Neeson, Roma Downey, Ciarán Hinds, and Kenneth Branagh. Northern Ireland also produced Christian intellectual and writer C. S. Lewis, Victorian physicist Lord Kelvin, engineer Harry Ferguson (inventor of the modern farm tractor and first four-wheel-drive Formula One car), and soccer-star playboy George Best—who once famously remarked, "I spent most of my money on liquor and women...and the rest I wasted."

As in the Republic, sports are big in the North. Northern-born golfers Rory McIlroy, Graeme McDowell, and Darren Clarke have won a fistful of majors, filling local hearts with pride. With close ties to Scotland, many Northern Irish fans follow the exploits of Glasgow soccer teams—but which team you root for betrays which side of the tracks you come from. Those who cheer for Glasgow Celtic (green and white) are Nationalist and Catholic; those waving banners for the Glasgow Rangers (blue with red trim) are Unionist and Protestant. To maintain peace, some pubs post signs on their doors banning patrons from wearing sports jerseys. Now sport teams with no sectarian history are popular, such as the Belfast Giants ice hockey team—a hit with both communities.

Northern Ireland is affordable, the roads are great, and it's small enough to get a real feel for the place on a short visit. Fishers flock to the labyrinth of lakes in County Fermanagh, hikers seek out County Antrim coastal crags, and those of Scots-Irish descent explore their ancestral farmlands (some of the best agricultural land on the island). Today, more tourists than ever are venturing north to Belfast and Derry, and cruise-ship crowds disembark in Belfast to board charter buses that fan out to visit the Giant's Causeway and Old Bushmills Distillery.

As you travel through Northern Ireland today, you'll encounter a fascinating country with a complicated, often tragic history—and a brightening future.

DERRY

No city in Ireland connects the kaleidoscope of historical dots more colorfully than Derry. From a leafy monastic hamlet to a Viking-pillaged port, from a cannonball-battered siege survivor to an Industrial Revolution sweatshop, from an essential WWII naval base to a wrenching flashpoint of sectarian Troubles... Derry has seen it all.

Though Belfast is the capital of Northern Ireland, this pivotal city has a more diverse history and a prettier setting. Derry was a vibrant city back when Belfast was just a mudflat. With less than half of Belfast's population (110,000), Derry feels more welcoming and manageable to visitors.

The town is the mecca of Ulster Unionism. When Ireland was being divvied up, the River Foyle was the logical border between Northern Ireland and the Republic. But, for sentimental and economic reasons, the North kept Derry, which is otherwise on the Republic's side of the river. Consequently, this predominantly Catholic-Nationalist city was much contested throughout the Troubles.

While most of its population and its city council call it "Derry," some maps, road signs, and all UK train schedules use "Londonderry," the name on its 1662 royal charter and the one favored by Unionists. I once asked a Northern Ireland rail employee for a ticket to "Derry"; he replied that there was no such place, but he would sell me one to "Londonderry." I'll call it Derry in this book since that's what the majority of the city's inhabitants do.

The past couple of decades have brought some refreshing changes. Manned British Army surveillance towers were taken down in 2006, and most British troops finally departed in mid-

2007, after 38 years in Northern Ireland. In 2011, a curvy pedestrian bridge across the River Foyle was completed. Locals dubbed it the Peace Bridge because it links the predominantly Protestant Waterside (east bank) with the predominantly Catholic Cityside (west bank). Today, you can feel comfortable wandering the streets and enjoying this underrated city.

PLANNING YOUR TIME

If just passing through (say, on your way to Portrush), it takes a few hours to see the essential Derry sights: Visit the Tower Museum and catch some views from the town wall.

With more time, spend a night in Derry, so you can see the powerful Bogside murals and take a walking tour around the town walls. With two nights in Derry, consider crossing back into the Republic for a scenic driving loop through part of remote County Donegal.

Orientation to Derry

The River Foyle flows north, slicing Derry into eastern and western chunks. The old town walls and almost all worthwhile sights are on the west side. (The tiny train station and Ebrington Square—at the end of the Peace Bridge—are the main reasons to spend time on the east side.) Waterloo Place and the adjacent Guildhall Square, just outside the north corner of the old city walls, are the pedestrian hubs of city activity. The Strand Road area extending north from Waterloo Place makes a comfortable home base, with lodging and restaurant suggestions within a block or two. The Diamond (main square) and its War Memorial statue mark the heart of the old city within the walls.

TOURIST INFORMATION

The TI, on Waterloo Place, can book bus and walking tours (Mon-Fri 9:00-17:30, Sat-Sun 10:00-17:00, closes earlier in off-season; 1 Waterloo Place, +44 28 7126 7284, www.visitderry.com).

ARRIVAL IN DERRY

By Train: Next to the river on the east side of town, Derry's little end-of-the-line train station (no storage lockers) has service to Portrush, Belfast, and Dublin. Each arriving train is greeted by free shuttle buses to Ulsterbus Station on the west side of town, a couple of minutes' walk south of Guildhall Square on Foyle Street (luggage storage at post office around corner in same building, Mon-Fri 9:30-17:30—beware of lunch closure, closed Sat-Sun). Otherwise, it's a £5 taxi ride to Guildhall Square. The same free shuttle service leaves Ulsterbus Station 15 minutes before each departing train.

DERRY

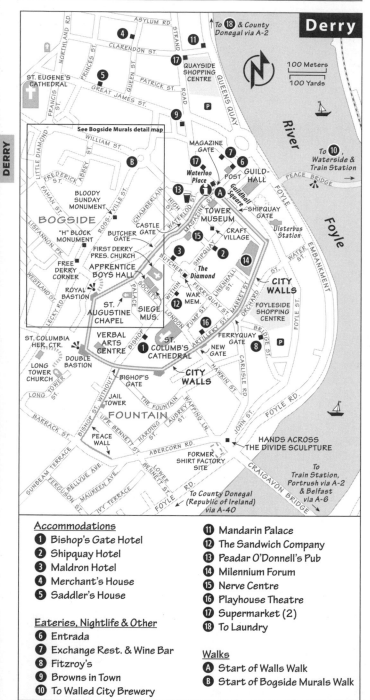

Derry

100 Meters

100 Yards

Accommodations

1 Bishop's Gate Hotel

2 Shipquay Hotel

3 Maldron Hotel

4 Merchant's House

5 Saddler's House

Eateries, Nightlife & Other

6 Entrada

7 Exchange Rest. & Wine Bar

8 Fitzroy's

9 Browns in Town

10 To Walled City Brewery

11 Mandarin Palace

12 The Sandwich Company

13 Peadar O'Donnell's Pub

14 Milennium Forum

15 Nerve Centre

16 Playhouse Theatre

17 Supermarket (2)

18 To Laundry

Walks

A Start of Walls Walk

B Start of Bogside Murals Walk

By Bus: All intercity buses stop at the Ulsterbus Station, on Foyle Street close to Guildhall Square.

By Car: The Foyleside parking garage by the Foyleside shopping center is handy for day-trippers (pay parking, check closing hours when you park). If staying overnight, ask about parking at your B&B, or try the parking garage at the Quayside shopping center (48 Strand Road; purchase overnight tickets from security desk in car park on arrival).

HELPFUL HINTS

Bookstore: Foyle Books is a dusty little pleasure for browsing (Mon-Fri 11:00-17:00, Sat 10:00-17:00, closed Sun, 12 Magazine Street at entrance to Craft Village, +44 28 7137 2530).

Laundry: Bubbles has drop-off service—bring it in the morning, pick up later that day (Mon-Fri 9:00-17:00, Sat from 10:00, closed Sun, 141 Strand Road, +44 28 7136 3366).

Taxi: Try **City Cabs** (+44 28 7126 4466), **The Taxi Company** (+44 28 7126 2626), or **Foyle Taxis** (+44 28 7127 9999).

Car Rental: Enterprise is handy (70 Clooney Road, +44 28 7186 1699, www.enterprise.co.uk). Another option is **Desmond Motors** (173 Strand Road, +44 28 7136 7136, www. desmondmotors.co.uk).

Tours in Derry

Walking Tours

McCrossan's City Tours leads insightful hour-long walks, giving a rounded view of the city's history. Tours depart from 11 Carlisle Road, just below Ferryquay Gate (£6; daily at 10:00, 12:00, 14:00, and 16:00; +44 28 7127 1996, mobile +44 77 1293 7997, www. derrycitytours.com, derrycitytours@icloud.com). They also offer private group tours.

Bogside History Tours offers walks led by Bogside residents who lost loved ones in the tragic events of Bloody Sunday (£10, daily at 11:00 and 13:00, departs from in front of the Guildhall, mobile +44 77 3145 0088, www.bogsidehistorytours.com, paul@ bogsidehistorytours.com). Tour guides also offer various taxi tours (£35/hour, call or email for options).

Bus Tours

Game of Thrones Tours brings you to the beautiful North Antrim Coast, focusing on locations used in the *Game of Thrones* TV series (see sidebar on page 50). Stops include Dunluce Castle (photo stop), Carrick-a-Rede Rope Bridge, Giant's Causeway, and the Dark Hedges (photo stop), with a lunch stop in Ballintoy (£40, Sat at 8:00 in summer, returns by 17:30, bus departs Derry

TI, no kids under 12, some walking, +44 28 9568 0023, www.gameofthronestours.com).

City Sightseeing's hop-on, hop-off double-decker buses are a good option for a general overview of Derry. The one-hour loop covers both sides of the river (seven stops overall), including the Guildhall, the old city walls, political wall murals, cathedrals, and former shirt factories. Your ticket is good for 24 hours (£15, pay driver, bus generally departs every 30-60 minutes daily 10:00-16:00 from in front of TI and Guildhall Square, +44 28 7151 1690, www.citysightseeingderry.com).

Walks in Derry

Though calm today, Derry is stamped by years of tumultuous conflict. These two self-guided walks (less than an hour each) explore the town's history. The "Walls Walk," starting on the old city walls and ending at the Anglican Cathedral, focuses on Derry's early days. My "Bogside Murals Walk" guides you to the city's compelling murals, which document the time of the Troubles. These walks, each worth ▲▲, can be done separately or linked, depending on your time.

WALLS WALK

Squatting determinedly in the city center, the old city walls of Derry (built 1613-1618 and still intact, except for wider gates to handle modern vehicles) hold an almost mythic place in Irish history.

It was here in 1688 that a group of brave apprentice boys, some of whom had been shipped to Derry as orphans after the great fire of London in 1666, made their stand. They slammed the city gates shut in the face of the approaching Catholic forces of deposed King James II. With this act, the boys galvanized the city's indecisive Protestant defenders inside the walls.

Months of negotiations and a grinding 105-day siege followed, during which a third of the 20,000 refugees and defenders crammed into the city perished. The siege was finally broken in 1689, when supply ships broke through a boom stretched across the River Foyle. The sacrifice and defiant survival of the city turned the tide in favor of newly crowned Protestant King William of Orange, who arrived in Ireland soon after and defeated James at the pivotal Battle of the Boyne.

To fully appreciate the walls, take a walk on top of them (free, open from dawn to dusk). Almost 20 feet high and at least as thick, the walls form a mile-long oval loop. The most interesting section is the half-circuit facing the Bogside, starting at Magazine Gate (stairs face the Tower Museum Derry inside the walls) and finishing at Bishop's Gate.

• *Enter the walls at Magazine Gate and find the stairs opposite the Tower Museum. Once atop the walls, head left.*

Walk the wall as it heads uphill, snaking along the earth's contours. In the row of buildings on the left (just before crossing over Castle Gate), you'll see an arch entry into the **Craft Village,** an alley lined with a cluster of cute shops and cafés that showcase the economic rejuvenation of Derry (Mon-Sat 9:30-17:30, closed Sun).

• *After crossing over Butcher Gate, stop in front of the grand building with the four columns to view the...*

First Derry Presbyterian Church: This impressive-looking building is the second church to occupy this site. The first was built by Queen Mary in the 1690s to thank the Presbyterian community for standing by their Anglican brethren during the dark days of the famous siege. That church was later torn down to make room for today's stately Neoclassical, red-sandstone church finished in 1780. Over the next 200 years, time took its toll on the structure, which was eventually closed due to dry rot and Republican firebombings. But in 2011, the renovated church reopened to a chorus of cross-community approval (yet one more sign of the slow reconciliation taking place in Derry). The **Blue Coat School** exhibit behind the church highlights the important role of Presbyterians in local history (free but donation encouraged, open summers only Wed-Fri 11:00-16:00, +44 28 7126 1550).

• *Just up the block is the...*

Apprentice Boys Memorial Hall: Built in 1873, this houses the private lodge and meeting rooms of an all-male Protestant organization. The group is dedicated to the memory of the original 13 apprentice boys who saved the day during the 1688 siege. Each year, on the Saturday closest to the August 12 anniversary date, the modern-day Apprentice Boys Society celebrates the end of the siege with a controversial march atop the walls. These walls are considered sacred ground for devout Unionists, who claim that many who died during the famous siege were buried within the battered walls because of lack of space. The **Siege Museum** stands behind the hall, giving a narrow-focus Unionist view of the siege (£5, Mon-Sat 10:00-17:00, closed Sun, last entry one hour before closing, 18 Society Street, +44 28 7126 1219).

Next, you'll pass a large, square pedestal on the right atop Royal Bastion. It once supported a column in honor of Governor

Derry's History

Once an island in the River Foyle, Derry (from *doire,* Irish for "oak grove") was chosen by St. Columba (St. Colmcille) around AD 546 for a monastic settlement. He later banished himself to the island of Iona in Scotland out of remorse for sparking a bloody battle over the rights to a holy manuscript that he had secretly copied.

A thousand years later, the English defeated the last Ulster-based Gaelic chieftains in the Battle of Kinsale (1601). With victory at hand, the English took advantage of the power vacuum. They began the "plantation" of Ulster with loyal Protestant subjects imported from Scotland and England. The native Irish were displaced to less desirable rocky or boggy lands, sowing the seeds of resentment that eventually fueled the Troubles.

A dozen wealthy London guilds (grocers, haberdashers, tailors, and others) took on Derry as an investment and changed its name to "Londonderry." They built the last great walled city in Ireland to protect their investment from the surrounding—and hostile—Irish locals. The walls proved their worth in 1688-1689, when the town's Protestant defenders, loyal to King William of Orange, withstood a prolonged siege by the forces of Catholic King James II. "No surrender" is still a passionate rallying cry among Ulster Unionists determined to remain part of the United Kingdom.

The town became a major port of emigration to the New World in the early 1800s. Then, when the Industrial Revolution provided a steam-powered sewing factory, the city developed a thriving shirtmaking industry. The factories here employed mostly Catholic women who flocked in from rural County Donegal. Although Belfast grew larger and wealthier, Unionists tightened their grip on "Londonderry" and the walls that they regarded with almost holy reverence. In 1921, they insisted that the city be included in Northern Ireland when the province was partitioned from the new Irish Free State (later to become the Republic of Ireland). A bit of gerrymandering (with three lightly populated Unionist districts outvoting two densely populated Nationalist

George Walker, the commander of the defenders during the siege. In 1972, the IRA blew up the column, which had 105 steps to the top (one for each day of the siege). An adjacent plaque shows a photo of the column before it was destroyed.

• *Opposite the empty pedestal is the small Anglican...*

St. Augustine Chapel: Set in a pretty graveyard, this Angli-

districts) ensured that the Protestant minority maintained control of the city, despite its Catholic majority.

Derry was a key escort base for US convoys headed for Britain during World War II, and 60 surviving German U-boats were instructed to surrender here at the end of the war. After the war, poor Catholics—unable to find housing—took over the abandoned military barracks, with multiple families living in each dwelling. Only homeowners were allowed to vote, and the Unionist minority, which controlled city government, was not eager to build more housing that would tip the voting balance away from them. Over the years, sectarian pressures gradually built—until they reached the boiling point. The ugly events of Bloody Sunday on January 30, 1972, brought worldwide attention to the Troubles (see the "Bloody Sunday" sidebar on page 24).

Today, life has stabilized in Derry, and the population has increased by 25 percent in the last 30 years. The 1998 Good Friday Peace Accord made significant progress toward peace, and the British Army withdrew 90 percent of its troops in mid-2007. With a population that is over 70 percent Catholic, the city has agreed to alternate Nationalist and Unionist mayors. There is a feeling of cautious optimism as Derry—the epicenter of bombs and bloody conflicts in the 1960s and 1970s—now boasts a history museum that airs all viewpoints.

The city continues to work on building a happier image. The wall—with all its troubled imagery and once nicknamed "the noose"—is now called "the necklace." With its complicated history, you're damned-if-you-do and damned-if-you-don't when it comes to calling it Derry (pro-Catholic, Nationalist) or Londonderry (pro-Protestant, Unionist). Some call it Derry/Londonderry or Londonderry/Derry. Others just say "Slashtown." And the tourist board calls it "legend-Derry."

can chapel is where some believe the original sixth-century monastery of St. Columba stood. The quaint grounds are open to visitors (Mon-Sat 10:30-16:30, closed Sun except for worship). In Victorian times, this stretch of the walls was a fashionable promenade walk.

As you walk, you'll pass a long wall (on the left)—all that's left of a former **British Army base,** which stood here until 2006.

Two 50-foot towers used to loom out of it, bristling with cameras and listening devices. Soldiers built them here for a bird's-eye view of the once-turbulent Catholic Bogside district below. The towers' dismantlement—as well as the removal of most of the British Army from Northern Ireland—is another positive sign in cautiously optimistic Derry. The walls of this former army base now contain a parking lot.

Stop at the **Double Bastion** fortified platform that occupies this corner of the city walls. The old cannon is nicknamed "Roaring Meg" for the fury of its firing during the siege.

From here, you can see across the Bogside to the not-so-faraway hills of County Donegal in the Republic. Derry was once an island, but as the River Foyle gradually changed its course, the area you see below the wall began to drain. Over time, and especially after the Great Potato Famine, Catholic peasants from rural Donegal began to move into Derry to find work during the Industrial Revolution. They settled on this least desirable land...on the soggy bog side of the city. From this vantage point, survey the Bogside with its political murals and Palestinian flags.

Directly below and to the right are Free Derry Corner and Rossville Street, where the tragic events of Bloody Sunday took place. Down on the left is the 18th-century Long Tower Catholic church, named after the monk-built round tower that once stood in the area (see listing under "Sights in Derry," later).

• *Head to the grand brick building behind you. This is the...*

Verbal Arts Centre: A former Presbyterian school, this center promotes the development of local literary arts in the form of poetry, drama, writing, and storytelling. Drop in or check the events schedule online (www.verbalartscentre.co.uk).

• *Go another 50 yards around the corner to reach...*

Bishop's Gate: From here, look up Bishop Street Within (inside the walls). This was the site of another British Army surveillance tower. Placed just inside the town walls, it overlooked the neighborhood until 2006. Now look in the other direction to see Bishop Street Without (outside the walls). You'll spot a modern wall topped by a high mesh fence, running along the left side of Bishop Street Without.

This is a so-called **"peace wall,"** built to ensure the security of the Protestant enclave living behind it in Derry's Fountain neighborhood. When the Troubles reignited over 50 years ago, 20,000 Protestants lived on this side of the river. This small housing development of 1,000 people is all that remains of that proud community today. The rest have chosen to move across the river to the mostly Protestant Waterside district. The stone tower halfway down the peace wall is all that remains of the old jail that briefly held doomed rebels after a 1798 revolt against the British.

• *From Bishop's Gate, those short on time can descend from the walls and walk 15 minutes directly back through the heart of the old city, along Bishop Street Within and Shipquay Street to Guildhall Square. With more time, consider visiting St. Columb's Cathedral, the Long Tower Church, and the murals of the Bogside.*

BOGSIDE MURALS WALK

The Catholic Bogside area was the tinderbox of the modern Troubles in Northern Ireland. Bloody Sunday, a terrible confrontation during a march that occurred nearly 50 years ago, sparked a sectarian inferno, and the ashes have not yet fully cooled. Today, the murals of the Bogside give visitors an accessible glimpse of this community's passionate perception of those events.

Getting There: The events are memorialized in 12 murals painted on the ends of residential flats along a 200-yard stretch of Rossville Street and Lecky Road, where the march took place. For the purposes of this walk, you can reach them from Waterloo Place via William Street. They are also accessible from the old city walls at Butcher Gate via the long set of stairs extending below Fahan Street on the grassy hillside, or by the stairs leading down from the Long Tower Church. These days, this neighborhood is gritty but quiet and safe.

The Artists: Two brothers, Tom and William Kelly, and their childhood friend Kevin Hasson are known as the Bogside Artists. They grew up in the Bogside and witnessed the tragic events that took place there, which led them to begin painting the murals in 1994. One of the brothers, Tom, gained a reputation as a "heritage mural" painter, specializing in scenes of life in the old days. In a surprising and hopeful development, Tom was later invited into Derry's Protestant Fountain neighborhood to work with a youth club there on three proud heritage murals that were painted over paramilitary graffiti.

The Murals: Start out at the roundabout intersection of Rossville and William streets.

The Bogside murals face different directions (and some are partially hidden by buildings), so they're not all visible from a single viewpoint. Plan on walking three long blocks along Rossville Street (which becomes Lecky Road) to see them all. Residents are used to visitors and don't mind if you photograph the murals. Local motorists are uncommonly courteous with allowing visitors to cross the busy street.

DERRY

From William Street, walk south along the right side of Rossville Street toward Free Derry Corner. The murals will all be on your right.

The first mural you'll walk past is the colorful ❶ *Peace,* showing the silhouette of a dove in flight (left side of mural) and an oak leaf (right side of mural), both created from a single ribbon. A peace campaign asked Derry city schoolchildren to write suggestions for positive peacetime images; their words inspired this artwork. The dove is a traditional symbol of peace, and the oak leaf is a traditional symbol of Derry—recognized by both communities. The dove flies from the sad blue of the past toward the warm yellow of the future.

❷ *The Hunger Strikers,* repainted during the summer of 2015, features two Derry-born participants of the 1981 Maze Prison hunger strike, as well as their mothers, who sacrificed and supported them in their fatal decision (10 strikers died). The prison was closed after the release of all prisoners (both Unionist and Nationalist) in 2000.

Smaller and easy to miss (above a ramp with banisters) is ❸ *John Hume.* It's actually a collection of four faces (clockwise from upper left): Nationalist leader John Hume, Martin Luther King, Jr., Nelson Mandela, and Mother Teresa. The Brooklyn Bridge in the middle symbolizes the long-term bridges of understanding that the work of these four Nobel Peace Prize-winning activists created. Born in the Bogside, Hume still maintains a home here.

Now look for ❹ *The Saturday Matinee,* which depicts an outgunned but undaunted local youth behind a screen shield. He holds a stone, ready to throw, while a British armored vehicle approaches (echoing the famous Tiananmen Square photo of the lone Chinese man facing the tank). Why *Saturday Matinee?* It's because the weekend was the best time for locals to engage in a little "recreational rioting" and "have a go at" the army; people were off work and youths were out of school. The "MOFD" at the bottom of this mural stands for the nearby Museum of Free Derry.

Nearby is ❺ *Civil Rights,* showing a marching Derry crowd carrying an anti-sectarian banner. It dates from the days when Martin Luther King, Jr.'s successful nonviolent marches were being

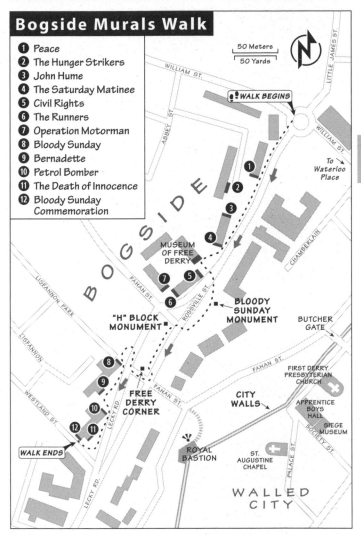

Bogside Murals Walk

1. Peace
2. The Hunger Strikers
3. John Hume
4. The Saturday Matinee
5. Civil Rights
6. The Runners
7. Operation Motorman
8. Bloody Sunday
9. Bernadette
10. Petrol Bomber
11. The Death of Innocence
12. Bloody Sunday Commemoration

50 Meters
50 Yards

WILLIAM ST.

WILLIAM ST.

WALK BEGINS

ABBEY ST.

To Waterloo Place

DERRY

B O G S I D E

CHAMBERLAIN

MUSEUM OF FREE DERRY

FAHAN ST.

ROSSVILLE ST.

BLOODY SUNDAY MONUMENT

BUTCHER GATE

LISFANNON PARK

LISFANNON

"H" BLOCK MONUMENT

FAHAN ST.

FIRST DERRY PRESBYTERIAN CHURCH

WESTLAND ST.

FREE DERRY CORNER

LECKY RD.

FAHAN ST.

CITY WALLS

APPRENTICE BOYS HALL

SIEGE MUSEUM

WALK ENDS

ROYAL BASTION

ST. AUGUSTINE CHAPEL

SOCIETY ST.

PALACE ST.

W A L L E D
C I T Y

seen worldwide on TV, creating a dramatic, global ripple effect. Civil rights marches, inspired by King and using the same methods to combat a similar set of grievances, gave this long-suffering community a powerful new voice.

All along this walk you'll notice lots of flags, including the red, black, white, and green Palestinian flag. Palestinians and Catholic residents of Northern Ireland have a special empathy for each other—both are indigenous people dealing with the persistent realities of sharing what they consider their rightful homeland with more powerful settlers planted there for political reasons.

Bloody Sunday

Inspired by civil rights marches in America in the mid-1960s, and the Prague Spring uprising and Paris student strikes of 1968, civil rights groups began to protest in Northern Ireland around this time. Initially, their goals were to gain better housing, secure fair voting rights, and end employment discrimination for Catholics in Northern Ireland. Tensions mounted, and clashes with the predominantly Protestant Royal Ulster Constabulary police force became frequent. Eventually, the British Army was called in to keep the peace.

On January 30, 1972, about 10,000 people protesting internment without trial held an illegal march sponsored by the Northern Ireland Civil Rights Association. British Army barricades kept them from the center of Derry, so they marched through the Bogside neighborhood.

That afternoon, some youths rioted on the fringe of the march. An elite parachute regiment had orders to move in and make arrests in the Rossville Street area. Shooting broke out, and after 25 minutes, 13 marchers were dead and 13 were wounded (one of the wounded later died). The soldiers claimed they came under attack from gunfire and nail-bombs. The marchers said the army shot indiscriminately at unarmed civilians.

The clash, called "Bloody Sunday," uncorked pent-up frustration as moderate Nationalists morphed into staunch Republicans overnight and released a flood of fresh IRA volunteers. An investigation at the time exonerated the soldiers, but the relatives of the victims called it a whitewash and insisted on their innocence.

In 1998, then-British Prime Minister Tony Blair promised a new inquiry, which became the longest and most expensive in British legal history. In 2010, a 12-year investigation—the Saville Report—determined that the Bloody Sunday civil rights protesters were innocent and called the deaths of 14 protesters unjustified.

In a dramatic 2010 speech in the House of Commons, then-British Prime Minister David Cameron apologized to the people of Derry. "What happened on Bloody Sunday was both unjustified and unjustifiable. It was wrong," he declared. Cheers rang out in Derry's Guildhall Square, where thousands had gathered to watch the televised speech. After 38 years, Northern Ireland's bloodiest wound started healing.

In the building behind this mural, you'll find the intense **Museum of Free Derry** (£7, Tue-Sat 10:00-16:00, closed Sun-Mon, 55 Glenfada Park, +44 28 7136 0880, www.museumoffreederry.org). Photos, shirts with bullet holes, and a video documentary convey Bogside residents' experiences during the worst of the Troubles. At the far end of the museum's outdoor wall (high up on the second floor of an adjacent residential building) is a copy of a famous painting by Francisco Goya depicting another massacre—this one in Spain—called the *Third of May 1808*. This reproduction draws a stark parallel to the local events that occurred here. Below and to the left of the painting (next to a gated alley) are two large bullet holes in the wall, inflicted on Bloody Sunday and preserved behind glass.

Cross over to the other side of Rossville Street to see the **Bloody Sunday Monument.** This small, fenced-off stone obe-

lisk lists the names of those who died that day, most within 50 yards of this spot. Take a look at the map pedestal by the monument, which shows how a rubble barricade was erected to block the street. A 10-story housing project called Rossville Flats stood here in those days. After peaceful protests failed (with Bloody Sunday being the watershed event), Nationalist youths became more aggressive. British troops were wary of being hit by Molotov cocktails thrown from the rooftop of the housing project.

Cross back again, this time over to the grassy median strip that runs down the middle of Rossville Street. At this end stands a granite letter *H* inscribed with the names of the IRA hunger strikers who died (and how many days they starved) in the H-block of Maze Prison (see *"The Hunger Strikers,"* earlier in the walk).

From here, as you look across at the corner of Fahan Street, you get a good view of two murals. In ❻ *The Runners* (right), four rioting youths flee tear gas from canisters used by the British Army to disperse hostile crowds. More than 1,000 canisters were used during the Battle of the Bogside; "nonlethal" rubber bullets killed 17 people over the course of the Troubles. Meanwhile, in ❼ *Operation Motorman* (left), a soldier wields a sledgehammer to break through a house door, depicting the massive push by the British Army to open up the Bogside's barricaded "no-go" areas that the

IRA had controlled for three years (1969-1972).

Walk down to the other end of the median strip where the white wall of **Free Derry Corner** announces "You are now entering Free Derry" (imitating a similarly defi-

DERRY

Political Murals

The dramatic and emotional murals you'll encounter in Northern Ireland will likely be one of your trip's most enduring travel memories. During the 19th century, Protestant neighborhoods hung flags and streamers each July to commemorate the victory of King William of Orange at the Battle of the Boyne in 1690. Modern murals evolved from these colorful annual displays. With the advent of industrial paints, temporary seasonal displays became permanent territorial statements.

Unionist murals were created during the extended Home Rule political debate that eventually led to the partitioning of the island in 1921 and the creation of Northern Ireland. Murals that expressed opposing views in Nationalist Catholic neighborhoods were outlawed. The ban remained until the eruption of the modern Troubles, when staunchly Nationalist Catholic communities isolated themselves behind barricades, eluding state control and gaining freedom to express their pent-up passions. In Derry, this form of symbolic, cultural, and ideological resistance first appeared in 1969 with the simple "You are now entering Free Derry" message that you'll still see painted on the surviving gable wall at Free Derry Corner.

Found mostly in working-class neighborhoods of Belfast and Derry, today's political murals have become a dynamic form of popular culture. They blur the line between art and propaganda, giving visitors a striking glimpse of each community's history, identity, and values.

ant slogan of the time in once-isolated West Berlin). This was the gabled end of a string of houses that stood here almost 50 years ago. During the Troubles, it became a traditional meeting place for speakers to address crowds. A portion of this mural changes from time to time, calling attention to injustice suffered by kindred spirits around the world (the plight of Palestinians and Basques are common themes).

Cross back to the right side of the street (now Lecky Road) to see ❽ *Bloody Sunday,* in which a small group of men carry a body from that ill-fated march. It's based on a famous photo of Father Edward Daly that was taken that day. Hunched over, he waves a white handkerchief to request safe passage in order to evacuate a mortally wounded protester. The bloodstained civil rights banner was inserted under the soldier's feet for extra emphasis. After

Bloody Sunday, the previously marginal IRA suddenly found itself swamped with bitterly determined young recruits.

Near it is a mural called ➒ *Bernadette.* The woman with the megaphone is Bernadette Devlin McAliskey, an outspoken civil rights leader, who, at age 21, became the youngest elected member of British Parliament. Behind her kneels a female supporter, banging a trash-can lid against the street in a traditional expression of protest in Nationalist neighborhoods. Trash-can lids were also used to warn neighbors of the approach of British patrols.

➓ *Petrol Bomber,* showing a teen wearing an army-surplus gas mask, captures the Battle of the Bogside, when locals barricaded their community, effectively shutting out British rule. Though the main figure's face is obscured by the mask, his body clearly communicates the resolve of an oppressed people. In the background, the long-gone Rossville Flats housing project still looms, with an Irish tricolor flag flying from its top.

In ⓫ *The Death of Innocence,* a young girl stands in front of bomb wreckage. She is Annette McGavigan, a 14-year-old who was killed on this corner by crossfire in 1971. She was the 100th fatality of the Troubles, which eventually took more than 3,000 lives (and she was also a cousin of one of the artists). The broken gun beside her points to the ground, signifying that it's no longer being wielded. The large butterfly above her shoulder symbolizes the hope for peace. For years, the artists left the butterfly an empty silhouette until they felt confident that the peace process had succeeded. They finally filled in the butterfly with optimistic colors in the summer of 2006.

Finally, around the corner, you'll see a circle of male faces. This mural, painted in 1997 to observe the 25th anniversary of the tragedy, is called ⓬ *Bloody Sunday Commemoration* and shows the 14 victims. They are surrounded by a ring of 14 oak leaves—the symbol of Derry. When relatives of the dead learned that the three Bogside Artists were beginning to paint this mural, many came forward to loan the artists precious photos of their loved ones, so they could be more accurately depicted.

While these murals preserve the struggles of the late 20th century, today sectarian violence has given way to negotiations and a settlement that seems to be working in fits and starts. The British apology for the Bloody Sunday shootings was a huge step forward. Former Nationalist leader John Hume (who shared the 1998 Nobel Peace Prize with then-Unionist leader David Trimble) once borrowed a quote from Gandhi to explain his nonviolent approach to the peace process: "An eye for an eye leaves everyone blind."

Sights in Derry

▲▲Tower Museum Derry

This well-organized museum combines modern audiovisual displays with historical artifacts to tell Derry's story from a skillfully unbiased viewpoint, sorting out some of the tangled history of Northern Ireland's Troubles. Occupying a modern reconstruction of a fortified medieval tower house that belonged to the local O'Doherty clan, it provides an excellent introduction to the city.

Cost and Hours: £4, includes audioguide for Armada exhibits, daily 9:00-17:30, last entry at 16:00, Union Hall Place, +44 28 7137 2411, www.derrystrabane.com/towermuseum.

Visiting the Museum: The museum is divided into two sections: the Story of Derry (on the ground floor) and the Spanish Armada (on the four floors of the tower).

Start with the **Story of Derry,** which explains the city's monastic origins 1,500 years ago. The exhibit moves through pivotal events, such as the 1688-1689 siege, as well as unexpected blips, like Amelia Earhart's emergency landing. Don't miss the thought-provoking 15-minute film in the small theater—it offers an even-handed local perspective on the tragic events of the modern sectarian conflict, giving you a better handle on what makes this unique city tick. Scan the displays of paramilitary paraphernalia in the hallway lined with colored curbstones—red, white, and blue Union Jack colors for Unionists; and the green, white, and orange Irish tricolor for Nationalists.

The tower section holds the **Spanish Armada** exhibits, filled with items taken from the wreck of *La Trinidad Valencera.* The ship sank off the coast of Donegal in 1588 in fierce storms nicknamed the "Protestant Winds." A third of the Armada's ships were lost in storms off the coasts of Ireland and Scotland. Survivors who made it ashore were hunted and killed by English soldiers. But a small number made it to Dunluce Castle (see page 51), where the sympathetic lord, who was no friend of the English, smuggled them to Scotland and eventual freedom in France.

Guildhall

This Neo-Gothic building, complete with clock tower, is the ceremonial seat of city government. Inside the hall are the Council Chamber, party offices, and an assembly hall featuring stained-glass windows showing scenes from Derry history.

Cost and Hours: Free, Mon-Fri 9:00-20:00, Sat-Sun until 18:00, last entry one hour before closing, free and clean WCs on ground floor, +44 28 7137 6510, www.derrystrabane.com/ guildhall.

Background: The Guildhall first opened in 1890 on reclaimed lands that were once the mudflats of the River Foyle. Destroyed by fire and rebuilt in 1913, it was massively damaged by IRA bombs in 1972. In an ironic twist, Gerry Doherty, one of those convicted of the bombings, was elected as a member of the Derry City Council a dozen years later.

Visiting the Hall: Take an informational pamphlet from the front window and explore, if civic and cultural events are not taking place inside. Rotating exhibits fill a ground-floor hall just to the right of the front reception desk. The Ulster Plantation exhibition is worth a visit. A mighty pipe organ fills much of a wall in the grand hall. It's lonely and loves to be played (if you would like to give it a go, just ask a guard).

On the back terrace, facing the river, you'll find locals lunching at the pleasant Guild Café (daily 9:30-17:00). And across the street is the modest but heartfelt Peace Park, with hopeful, nonsectarian children's quotes on tiles that line the path.

Peace Bridge Stroll

Stroll across the architecturally fetching Peace Bridge for great views over the river toward the city center (best at sunset). The €14 million pedestrian Peace Bridge opened in 2011, linking neighborhoods long divided by the river (Catholic Nationalists on the west bank and Protestant Unionists on the east bank). On the far side from the old city walls, the former Ebrington Barracks British Army base (1841-2003) sits on prime real estate and surrounds a huge square that was once the military parade ground. This area features a fun gastropub, and serves as an outdoor concert venue and community gathering spot. Plans are in progress to develop this area further with a hotel and museum complex.

Hands Across the Divide

Designed by local teacher Maurice Harron, this powerful metal sculpture of two figures extending their hands to each other was

inspired by the growing hope for peace and reconciliation in Northern Ireland (located at roundabout at west end of Craigavon Bridge).

The Tillie and Henderson's shirt factory (opened in 1857 and burned down in 2003) once stood on the banks of the river beside the bridge, looming over the figures. In its heyday, Derry's shirt industry employed more than 15,000 workers (90 percent of whom were women) in sweathouses typical of the human toll of the Industrial Revolution. Karl Marx mentioned this factory in *Das Kapital* as an example of women's transition from domestic to industrial work lives.

St. Columb's Cathedral

Marked by the tall spire inside the walls, this was the first Protestant cathedral built in Britain after the Reformation. St. Columb's played an important part in the defense of the city during the siege. During that time, cannons were mounted on its roof, and the original spire was scavenged for lead to melt into cannon shot. This Anglican cathedral was built from 1628 to 1633 in a style called "Planter's Gothic," financed by the same London companies that backed the Protestant plantation of Londonderry.

Cost and Hours: £2 donation, Mon-Sat 9:00-17:00, closed Sun, +44 28 7126 7313, www.stcolumbscathedral.org.

Visiting the Cathedral: Before you enter, walk over to the "Heroes' Mound" at the end of the churchyard closest to the town wall. Underneath this grassy dome is a mass grave of some of those who died during the 1689 siege.

In the cathedral entryway, you'll find a hollow cannonball that was lobbed into the city—it contained the besiegers' surrender terms. Inside, along the nave, hangs a musty collection of battle flags and Union Jacks that once inspired troops during the siege, the Crimean War, and World War II.

An American flag hung among them until a few years ago when its gradual deterioration prompted its current storage under glass (viewable in wooden case to right of front altar—fourth drawer from top). It's from the time when the first GIs to enter the European theater in World War II were based in Northern Ireland.

To the left of the front altar is a seven-minute video covering the cathedral's history. Check out the small chapter-house museum in the back of the church to see the huge original locks of the gates of Derry and more relics of the siege.

Long Tower Church

Built below the walls on the hillside above the Bogside, this modest-looking church is worth a visit for its stunning high altar. The name comes from a stone monastic round tower that stood here for centuries but was dismantled and used for building materials in the 1600s.

Cost and Hours: Free, generally open Mon-Sat 8:30-20:30, Sun 7:30-18:00, +44 28 7126 2301, www.longtowerchurch.org.

Visiting the Church: Long Tower Church, the oldest Catholic church in Derry, was finished in 1786, during a time of enlightened relations between the city's two religious communities. Protestant Bishop Hervey gave a generous-for-the-time £200 donation and had the four Corinthian columns shipped in from Naples to frame the Neo-Renaissance altar.

Outside, walk behind the church and face the Bogside to find a simple shrine hidden beneath a hawthorn tree. It marks the spot where outlawed Masses were secretly held before this church was built, during the Penal Law period of the early 1700s. Through the Penal Laws, the English attempted to weaken Catholicism's influence by banishing priests and forbidding Catholics from buying land, attending school, voting, and holding office.

Nearby: The adjacent **St. Columba Heritage Centre** fleshes out the life of Derry's patron saint and founding father (£3, Mon-Fri 10:00-16:00, Sat-Sun from 13:00, closed Mon in winter, +44 28 7136 8491, www.stcolumbaheritage.com).

Nightlife in Derry

The **Millennium Forum** is a modern venue that reflects the city's revived investment in local culture, concerts, and plays (box office open Mon-Sat 9:30-17:00, inside city walls on Newmarket Street near Ferryquay Gate, +44 28 7126 4455, www.millenniumforum.co.uk).

The **Nerve Centre** hosts a wide variety of art-house films and live concerts (inside city walls at 7 Magazine Street, near Butcher Gate, +44 28 7126 0562, www.nervecentre.org).

The **Playhouse Theatre** is an intimate venue for plays, music, and readings (£7-20 tickets, inside walls on Artillery Street, between New Gate and Ferryquay Gate, +44 28 7126 8027, www.derryplayhouse.co.uk).

To mingle with Derry's friendly conversational residents, try

Peadar O'Donnell's pub on Waterloo Street for the city's best nightly traditional music sessions (music often starts late—around 23:00, 53 Waterloo Street, +44 28 7137 2318).

Sleeping in Derry

The first three options are located inside the city's walls and feature all the modern comforts. The others are in historic buildings with creaky charm and friendly hosts.

$$$$ Bishop's Gate Hotel is Derry's top lodging option and priced that way. This former gentlemen's club, once frequented by Winston Churchill, has 31 rooms that ooze with cushy refinement (no breakfast, gym, fine bar, 24 Bishop Street, +44 28 7114 0300, www.bishopsgatehotelderry.com, sales@bishopsgatehotelderry.com). They also rent one apartment (sleeps 4).

$$$$ The **Shipquay Hotel,** in a former bank building that dates to 1895, rents 21 handsome rooms, some with wall views. The Lock & Quay cocktail bar and a restaurant occupy the ground floor (no breakfast, 15 Shipquay Street, +44 28 7126 7266, www. shipquayhotel.com, info@shipquayhotel.com).

$$ Maldron Hotel features 93 modern, bright, and large rooms, some overlooking the city walls and Bogside. It also has a restaurant, bar, and 20 private basement parking spaces (breakfast extra, family rooms, gym, sauna, laundry service, Butcher Street, +44 28 7137 1000, www.maldronhotelderry.com, reservations. derry@maldronhotels.com).

$ Merchant's House, on a quiet street a 10-minute stroll from Waterloo Place, is a fine Georgian townhouse with a grand, color-ful drawing room and eight rooms sporting marble fireplaces and ornate plasterwork (family room, 16 Queen Street, +44 28 7126 9691, www.thesaddlershouse.com, saddlershouse@btinternet. com). Joan and Peter Pyne also run the Saddler's House (see below), and offer appealing self-catering townhouse rentals inside the walls (great for families or anyone needing extra space, 3-night minimum).

$ Saddler's House is a charming Victorian townhouse with seven rooms located a couple of blocks closer to the old town walls. Their muscular bulldog Bruno provides lovable comic relief (laundry service, 36 Great James Street, +44 28 7126 9691, www. thesaddlershouse.com, saddlershouse@btinternet.com).

Eating in Derry

$$$ Entrada is a crisp, modern restaurant with a faintly Span-ish theme, serving great meals, tapas, and fine wines in a posh, calm space. It faces the river a block from the Guildhall (Wed-Sat

12:00-21:30, Sun until 20:00, closed Mon-Tue, Queens Quay, +44 28 7137 3366).

$$$ Exchange Restaurant and Wine Bar offers hearty lunches and quality dinners with flair, in a central location near the river behind Waterloo Place (Mon-Fri 12:00-14:30 & 17:30-22:00, Sat 17:00-22:00, Sun 14:00-20:00, Queen's Quay, +44 28 7127 3990).

$$$ Fitzroy's, a family-run bistro tucked below Ferryquay Gate and stacked with locals, serves good lunches and dinners (Mon-Sat 12:00-22:00, Sun until 21:00, 2 Bridge Street, +44 28 7126 6211).

$$ Browns in Town is a casual, friendly lunch or dinner option near most of my recommended lodgings (Mon-Sat 12:00-15:00 & 17:30-21:00, Sun 17:00-21:00, 21 Strand Road, +44 28 7136 2889).

$$ Walled City Brewery, across the Peace Bridge, is a fun change of pace. The brewpub ambience and dependable comfort food can be washed down with a local fave: Derry chocolate milk stout (Wed-Thu 17:00-22:30, Fri-Sun 13:00-21:30, closed Mon-Tue, 70 Ebrington Square, +44 28 7134 3336).

$ Mandarin Palace is crowded with loyal locals eating filling Chinese fare; easy takeout is available (Mon-Sat 16:00-23:00, Sun from 13:00, Queens Quay, +44 28 7137 3656).

$ The Sandwich Company is a cheap and easy lunch counter and coffee shop in the center of the old town walls (Mon-Sat 8:00-17:30, Thu-Fri until 19:00, Sun 10:00-17:00, 6 Bishop Street Within, +44 28 7137 2500).

Supermarkets: You'll find everything you need for picnics at **Tesco** (Mon-Fri 8:00-21:00, Sat until 19:00, Sun 13:00-18:00, corner of Strand Road and Clarendon Street) or **SuperValu** (Mon-Sat 8:30-19:00, Sun 12:30-17:30, Waterloo Place).

Derry Connections

From Derry, it's an hour's drive to Portrush. If you're using public transportation, consider a Zone 4 iLink smartcard, good for all-day train and bus use in Northern Ireland (see page 59). Keep in mind that some bus and train schedules, road signs, and maps may say "Londonderry" or "L'Derry" instead of "Derry."

From Derry by Train to: Portrush (16/day, 1.5 hours, usually change in Coleraine), **Belfast** (16/day, 2 hours), **Dublin** (6/day, 4 hours, change in Belfast).

By Bus to: Galway (6/day, 5.5 hours), **Westport** (3/day, 6 hours, bus #64 to Knock Airport or Charleston then bus #440 to Derry), **Portrush** (5/day, 1.5 hours, change in Coleraine), **Belfast** (hourly, 2 hours), **Dublin** (12/day, 4 hours).

Near Derry

DERRY

▲Ulster American Folk Park

This combination museum and folk park (in a wonderfully scenic and walkable rural forest) explores the experiences of the many Irish who left their homeland during the hard times of the 18th century.

Cost and Hours: £9, book online in advance; Tue-Sun 10:00-17:00, shorter hours in winter, closed Mon year-round; cafeteria and picnic area, 2 Mellon Road, Omagh, +44 28 8224 3292, www.nmni.com.

Getting There: The folk park is in Omagh, 48 kilometers (30 miles) south of Derry on A-5—about a 45-minute drive.

Visiting the Park: Your visit starts with the excellent museum. From there, you'll head outdoors to see authentic shops and buildings from rural Ulster, as well as traditional craft demonstrations (before emigration). You can also board a full-scale emigrant ship and see some typical businesses and homes in the New World. You'll gain insight into the origins of the tough Scots-Irish stock— think Davy Crockett (his people were from Derry) and Andrew Jackson (Carrickfergus roots)—who later shaped America's westward migration. You'll also find good coverage of the *Titanic* tragedy, and its effect on the Ulster folk who built the ship and the loved ones it left behind.

Nearby: The adjacent **Mellon Centre for Migration Studies** is handy for genealogy searches (Tue-Fri 10:00-16:00, Sat from 11:00, closed Sun-Mon, +44 28 8225 6315, www.qub.ac.uk/cms).

PORTRUSH &
THE ANTRIM COAST

The Antrim Coast—the north of Northern Ireland—is one of the most interesting and scenic coastlines in Ireland. Portrush, at the end of the train line, is an ideal base for exploring the highlights of the Antrim Coast. Within a few miles of town, you can visit evocative castle ruins, tour the world's oldest whiskey distillery, catch a thrill on a bouncy rope bridge, and hike along the famous Giant's Causeway.

PLANNING YOUR TIME

You need a full day to explore the Antrim Coast, so allow two nights in Portrush. The main sights on the coast are the Giant's Causeway, Old Bushmills Distillery, Carrick-a-Rede Rope Bridge, and Dunluce Castle. Visiting all four is doable with a car in one busy day. Without a car, you can ride buses and hire taxis (see "Getting Around the Antrim Coast," next page), but time will be tight, so be selective. Add a third night if you plan to take longer hikes and/or visit Rathlin Island (book ahead for summer ferries).

In peak season (mid-June to mid-September), booking ahead is important if you want to cross the Carrick-a-Rede Rope Bridge, tour Bushmills Distillery, and do the official Giant's Causeway Visitor Experience (which includes access to the visitors center, parking, and an audioguide or guided tour). To fit it all in, select entry/tour times strategically when booking. You'll need at least two hours at Giant's Causeway, and 1-1.5 hours each at Bushmills and Carrick-a-Rede, plus travel time. It's about 15 minutes by car from Portrush to Bushmills, then 5 minutes from Bushmills to Giant's Causeway, and 20 minutes from there to Carrick-a-Rede.

Without reservations, you can still experience these sights

(and maintain some flexibility in your day). You can hike to Giant's Causeway on your own, and you can walk the scenic cliff-top path to see the Carrick-a-Rede Rope Bridge (but you won't be able to cross it). Dunluce Castle is the least crowded of the sights and can be toured quickly.

If driving on to Belfast from Portrush, consider the slower but scenic coastal route via the Glens of Antrim (see page 54).

GETTING AROUND THE ANTRIM COAST

By Car: A car is the best way to explore the charms of the Antrim Coast. Distances are short and parking is easy.

By Bus: In peak season, an all-day bus pass helps you get around the region economically. The **Causeway Rambler** (Ulsterbus #402) links Portrush with Dunluce Castle (10 minutes), Bushmills (15 minutes), Giant's Causeway (20 minutes), Dunseverick Castle (25 minutes), Carrick-a-Rede Rope Bridge (stopping at the nearby town of Ballintoy, 40 minutes), and Ballycastle (Rathlin Island ferry, 50 minutes). The bus costs £9.50/day and runs roughly 9:00-18:00 (8/day, fewer on Sun, check schedule at www.translink.co.uk, buy ticket from driver). In Portrush, the Rambler stops at Dunluce Avenue (a two-minute walk from the train station).

By Bus Tour: If you're based in Belfast, you can visit most of the sights on the Antrim Coast with a **McComb's** tour (see page 65).

By Taxi: Groups (up to four) can reasonably visit most sights by taxi (except the more distant Carrick-a-Rede and Rathlin Island sailings from Ballycastle). You'll pay metered fares; from Portrush, expect to pay these one-way prices: £10 (Dunluce Castle), £12 (Old Bushmills Distillery), £15 (Giant's Causeway), and £25-30 (Carrick-a-Rede). Try **Andy Brown's Taxi** (with a fleet of drivers, +44 28 7082 2223, https://andybrowntaxis.co.uk), **Hugh's Taxi** (mobile +44 77 0298 6110), **Gaz Cabs** (+44 77 0909 2737), or **S B Taxis** (multiple drivers but based in Coleraine, so rides may be longer and pricier, +44 28 7035 6560). See VisitPortrush.co.uk for a list of companies (on the "Services" tab), or search "taxis" in Google Maps for taxi services near your location.

Portrush

Homey Portrush used to be known as "the Brighton of the North." It first became a resort in the late 1800s, as railroads expanded to offer the new middle class a weekend by the shore. Victorians flocked here, believing that swimming in saltwater would cure many common ailments.

While not what it was in its heyday, Portrush retains the atmosphere and architecture of a genteel seaside resort. Its peninsula is filled with lowbrow, family-oriented amusements, fun eateries, and B&Bs. Summertime fun seekers promenade along the tiny harbor and tumble down to the sandy beaches, which extend in sweeping white crescents on either side.

Superficially, Portrush has the appearance of any small British seaside resort, but its history and large population of young people (students from nearby University of Ulster at Coleraine) give the town a little more personality. Along with the usual arcade amusements, there are nightclubs, restaurants, summer theater productions in the Town Hall, and convivial pubs that attract customers all the way from Belfast.

PORTRUSH & ANTRIM COAST

Orientation to Portrush

Portrush's pleasant and easily walkable town center features sea views in every direction. On one side are the harbor and many restaurants, and on the other are Victorian townhouses and vast, salty vistas. The tip of the peninsula features a recreational park area.

The town is busy with students during the school year. Summer (around mid-June to mid-September) is beach-resort boom time. There's a brief but intense spike in visitors in mid-May for a huge annual motorcycle race and on Easter weekend (see "Crowd Alert," later). Families pack Portrush on Saturdays, and revelers from Belfast crowd its hotels on Saturday nights.

Tourist Information: The TI is located underneath the central, red-brick Town Hall (Mon-Sat 9:00-17:00, Sun 11:00-16:00, closed off-season, Kerr Street, +44 28 7082 3333). Pick up the free *Visitor Guide* brochure.

Arrival in Portrush: The train tracks stop at the base of the tiny peninsula that Portrush fills (there's a small modern station but no baggage storage). Most of my recommended accommodations are within a 10-minute walk of the train station. The bus stop is two blocks from the train station.

Crowd Alert: Over a four-day weekend in mid-May, thousands of die-hard motorcycle fans converge on Portrush, Port Stewart, and Coleraine to watch the **Northwest 200 Race.** Fearless racers scorch the roads at 200 miles per hour on the longest straightaway in motorsports. Accommodations fill up a year ahead,

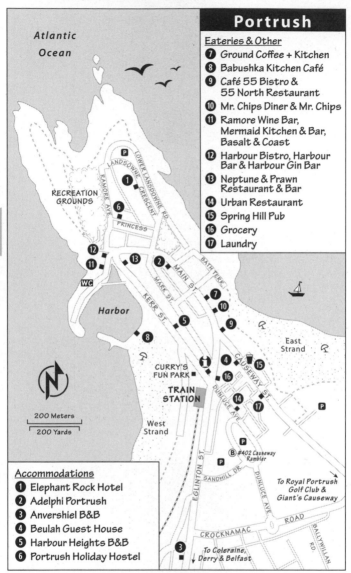

Portrush

Eateries & Other
- ❼ Ground Coffee + Kitchen
- ❽ Babushka Kitchen Café
- ❾ Café 55 Bistro & 55 North Restaurant
- ❿ Mr. Chips Diner & Mr. Chips
- ⓫ Ramore Wine Bar, Mermaid Kitchen & Bar, Basalt & Coast
- ⓬ Harbour Bistro, Harbour Bar & Harbour Gin Bar
- ⓭ Neptune & Prawn Restaurant & Bar
- ⓮ Urban Restaurant
- ⓯ Spring Hill Pub
- ⓰ Grocery
- ⓱ Laundry

Accommodations
- ❶ Elephant Rock Hotel
- ❷ Adelphi Portrush
- ❸ Anvershiel B&B
- ❹ Beulah Guest House
- ❺ Harbour Heights B&B
- ❻ Portrush Holiday Hostel

Atlantic Ocean

RECREATION GROUNDS

Harbor

West Strand

East Strand

CURRY'S FUN PARK

TRAIN STATION

#402 Causeway Rambler

To Royal Portrush Golf Club & Giant's Causeway

To Coleraine, Derry & Belfast

200 Meters
200 Yards

PORTRUSH & ANTRIM COAST

and traffic is the pits (dates and details at www.northwest200.org). Avoid visiting during crowded **Easter weekend.**

Laundry: Full service is available at **Causeway Laundry** (Mon-Tue and Thu-Fri 9:00-16:30, Wed and Sat until 13:00, closed Sun, drop off by 11:00 for same-day service, they can deliver cleaned clothes to nearby hotels, 68 Causeway Street, +44 28 7082 2060).

Activities in Portrush

Curry's Fun Park

Located just below the train station on the harbor, this fun arcade and amusement park offers a chance to see Northern Ireland at play. Older locals visit for the nostalgia, as many of the rides and amusements go back 50 years. Ride prices are listed at the door. Everything runs with tokens, and the place is bigger than it looks. Try some "candy floss" (cotton candy) or other sweet treat (daily until late in summer, weekends only in shoulder season, closed off-season, www.currysfunpark.com).

Royal Portrush Golf Club

Irish courses, like those in Scotland, are highly sought after for their lush greens in glorious settings. Serious golfers can get a tee time at the Royal Portrush, a links course that hosted the British Open in 1951 and 2019 (it's next set to host in 2025). Check out the trophy case and historic photos in the clubhouse (green fees generally £255, less most days in off-season). The adjacent, slightly shorter Valley Course is more budget-friendly (green fees £60, +44 28 7082 2311, www.royalportrushgolfclub.com).

Portrush Recreation Grounds

At the tip of the peninsula, this park is currently under redevelopment and will feature a bowling green, play area, a pavilion, and green space.

Sleeping in Portrush

Summer can be crowded (and loud) with young party groups, as are Saturday nights the rest of the year.

$$$$ Elephant Rock Hotel, on a street facing the waterfront, adds a punch of color to the Portrush landscape. The 18 rooms—all done up in various colorful versions of the hotel's "Art Deco glam" style—are wonderfully spacious, and some have sea views. The back terrace bar and front-of-house restaurant are as fun as the rooms (elevator, 17 Lansdowne Crescent, +44 28 7087 8787, www.elephantrockhotel.co.uk, info@elephantrockhotel.co.uk).

$$$$ Adelphi Portrush is one of the larger hotels in town, with 28 tastefully furnished rooms, an ideal location, and a hearty bistro downstairs (family rooms, 67 Main Street, +44 28 7082 5544, www.adelphiportrush.com, stay@adelphiportrush.com).

$$ Anvershiel B&B, with seven nicely refurbished rooms, is a great value and well-cared for. It's a pleasant 10-minute walk from the main part of town (RS%, family rooms, parking in front, 16 Coleraine Road, +44 73 9131 6246, www.anvershiel.com, anvershiel154@outlook.com, brother and sister Ian and Joanne).

$$ Beulah Guest House has 13 modern, clean-cut rooms in a fine central location (family room, save money by opting out of breakfast, parking at rear, 16 Causeway Street, +44 28 7082 2413, www.beulahguesthouse.com, stay@beulahguesthouse.com, Lorraine and Teresa).

$$ Harbour Heights B&B rents nine retro-homey rooms, each named after a different town in County Antrim. Its breakfast room, overlooking the harbor, is supervised by two cats. Friendly South African hosts Sam and Tim Swart manage the place with a light hand (family rooms, 17 Kerr Street, +44 28 7082 2765, mobile +44 78 9586 6534, www.harbourheightsportrush.com, harbourheightsportrush@gmail.com).

¢ Portrush Holiday Hostel offers clean, well-organized, economical lodging. With 11 rooms and no more than 40 guests, this is a small, intimate hostel (nice private rooms available, +44 28 7082 1288, mobile +44 78 5037 7367, 24 Princess Street, www.portrushholidayhostel.com, portrushholidayhostel@gmail.com).

Eating in Portrush

As a family getaway from Belfast and a beach escape for students from the nearby university in Coleraine, Portrush has more than enough fish-and-chips joints. And in recent years, the refined tastes of affluent golfers and urban professionals out for a weekend have prompted the town to up its culinary game.

LUNCH SPOTS

$ Ground Coffee + Kitchen serves breakfast all day, plus fresh sandwiches and paninis, soup, and great coffee (daily 8:30-17:30, July-Aug until 22:00, 52 Main Street, +44 28 7082 5979).

$ Babushka Kitchen Café, located on the pier, offers a small, creative menu of breakfast, lunch, and baked treats. Order at the walk-up window, then take your food for a stroll, or eat at one of a few tables (daily 9:15-17:00, West Strand Promenade, +44 77 8750 2012).

$$ Café 55 Bistro is an order-at-the-counter place with breakfast till noon, plus burgers, pizza, paninis, and a case of sweets. Their patio tables have great views (daily 9:00-17:00, until 21:00 in summer, 1 Causeway Street, beneath fancier 55 North restaurant, +44 28 7082 2811).

$ Mr. Chips Diner and **Mr. Chips** are the local favorites for cheap, quality fish-and-chips (Mon-Thu 12:00-21:00, Fri-Sun until 22:00, 12 and 20 Main Street). Both are mostly takeout, but the diner also has tables.

Groceries: For picnic supplies, try **Spar Market** (daily until late in summer, across from Curry's Fun Park on Main Street, +44 28 7082 5447).

HARBOR-SIDE EATERIES

A diverse and lively cluster of restaurants, all with the same owner, overlooks the harbor. Ramore Wine Bar, Mermaid, Basalt, and Coast share a building; Harbour Bistro and Neptune & Prawn are nearby. They all have a creative and fun energy, and are often jammed with diners. Most serve dinner only, and reservations are important in peak season. The most walk-in friendly are Ramore Wine Bar and Coast. Closed days may shift depending on staffing and demand (call ahead to check). You can make reservations at this shared website: RamoreRestaurant.com.

$$ Ramore Wine Bar is a salty, modern place, with an inviting menu ranging from steaks to vegetarian items. It's very casual but with serious cuisine. Order at the bar and take a table (open daily for lunch and dinner, +44 28 7082 4313).

$$$ Harbour Bistro is dark, noisy, and sprawling with a sloppy crowd enjoying chargrilled meat and fish at booths and bartop tables (closed Mon, +44 28 7082 2430).

$$ Mermaid Kitchen & Bar is all about fresh fish dishes with a Spanish twist and great harbor views. Those at the bar get a bird's-eye view of the fun banter and precision teamwork of the kitchen staff (closed Mon-Tue, +44 28 7082 6969).

$$ Basalt has Spanish-influenced small plates, a sophisticated hotel-bar vibe, top-floor views, and an outdoor terrace (closed Mon-Wed, +44 28 7082 6969).

$$ Neptune & Prawn (just across the inlet from the others) is the most yacht-clubby of the bunch. Serving Asian and other international food, with fancy presentation and many plates designed to be shared, this place is noisy and high energy (closed Mon-Tue, +44 28 7082 2448).

$$ Coast, a youthful family-friendly place, serves up pizzas, pastas, and burgers. In summer, they occasionally offer a bottomless food and drink special—call to ask about it (closed Mon-Tue, +44 28 7082 4313).

OTHER DINING OPTIONS

$$$ 55 North (named for the local latitude), on the other side of the peninsula from the harbor-facing eateries, has the best sea views, with windows on three sides. The filling fish dishes, along with some Asian plates, are a joy (open daily for lunch and dinner in summer, dinner only in off-season, reservations smart, 1 Causeway Street, +44 28 7082 2811, www.55-north.com).

$$ Urban Restaurant is not on the water and has no views, but the industrial modern dining room has good energy and the

PORTRUSH & ANTRIM COAST

The Scottish Connection

The Romans called the Irish the "Scoti" (meaning pirates). When the Scoti crossed the narrow Irish Sea and invaded the land of the Picts 1,500 years ago, that region became known as Scotland. Ireland and Scotland were never conquered by the Romans, and they retained similar clannish Celtic traits. Both share the same Gaelic branch of the linguistic tree.

On clear summer days from Carrick-a-Rede, the island of Mull in Scotland—only 17 miles away—is visible. Much closer on the horizon is the boomerang-shaped Rathlin Island, part of Northern Ireland. Rathlin is where Scottish leader Robert the Bruce (a compatriot of William "Braveheart" Wallace) retreated in 1307 after defeat at the hands of the English. Legend has it that he hid in a cave on the island, where he observed a spider patiently rebuilding its web each time a breeze knocked it down. Inspired by the spider's perseverance, Robert gathered his Scottish forces once more and finally defeated the English at the decisive Battle of Bannockburn.

Flush with confidence from his victory, Robert the Bruce decided to open a second front against the English...in Ireland. In 1315, he sent his brother Edward over to enlist their Celtic Irish cousins in an effort to thwart the English. After securing Ireland, Edward hoped to move on and enlist the Welsh, thus cornering England with their pan-Celtic nation. But Edward's timing was bad—Ireland was in the midst of famine. His Scottish troops had to live off the land and began to take food and supplies from the starving Irish. He might also have been trying to destroy Ireland's crops to keep them from being used as a colonial "breadbasket" to feed English troops. The Scots quickly wore out their welcome, and Edward the Bruce was eventually killed in battle near Dundalk in 1318.

This was the first time in history that Ireland was used as a pawn by England's enemies. Spain and France saw Ireland as the English Achilles' heel, and both countries later attempted invasions of the island. The English Tudor and Stuart royalty countered these threats in the 16th and 17th centuries by starting the "plantation" of loyal subjects in Ireland. The only successful long-term settlement by the English was here in Northern Ireland, which remains part of the United Kingdom today.

It's interesting to imagine how things might be different today if Ireland and Scotland had been permanently welded together as a nation 700 years ago. You'll notice the strong Scottish influence in this part of Ireland when you ask a local a question and he answers, "Aye, a wee bit." The Irish joke that the Scots are just Irish people who couldn't swim home.

food—burgers, seafood, meat, and Asian-influenced dishes—is solid (open daily for lunch and dinner, reservations smart, 26 Dunluce Avenue, +44 28 7051 1332, www.urbanportrush.com).

PUBS

Harbour Bar is an old-fashioned pub next to the Harbour Bistro (see earlier). **Harbour Gin Bar** (above Harbour Bar) is a rustic, spacious, and inviting place with live acoustic folk music at night and a fun selection of Irish gins.

Neptune & Prawn Cocktail Bar (above the restaurant by the same name; see listing earlier) has great views over the harbor and is the most classy yet inviting place in town for a drink (they also serve small plates).

Spring Hill Pub is a good bet for its friendly vibe and occasional live music, including traditional sessions Thursdays around 20:00 (17 Causeway Street, +44 28 7082 3361).

Portrush Connections

Consider a £16.50 Zone 4 iLink smartcard, good for all-day Translink train and bus use in Northern Ireland (www.translink.co.uk).

From Portrush by Train to: Coleraine (hourly, 12 minutes), **Belfast** (hourly, 1.5 hours, transfer in Coleraine), **Dublin** (7/day, 5 hours, transfer in Belfast). Note that on Sundays, service is greatly reduced.

By Bus to: Belfast (12/day, 2 hours; scenic coastal route, 2.5 hours), **Dublin** (4/day, 5.5 hours).

Antrim Coast

The craggy 20-mile stretch of the Antrim Coast extending eastward from Portrush to Ballycastle rates second only to the tip of the Dingle Peninsula as the prettiest chunk of coastal Ireland. From your base in Portrush, you have a grab bag of sightseeing choices: Giant's Causeway, Old Bushmills Distillery, Dunluce Castle, Carrick-a-Rede Rope Bridge, and Rathlin Island.

It's easy to weave these sights together by car, but connections are patchy by public transportation. Bus service is viable only in summer, and taxi fares are reasonable only for the sights closest to Portrush (Dunluce Castle, Old Bushmills Distillery, and the Giant's Causeway). For details on how to plan your day on the Antrim Coast, and for more on your transportation options, see "Planning Your Time" and "Getting Around the Antrim Coast," at the beginning of this chapter.

Eating Along the Antrim Coast: Both Bushmills Distillery and the Giant's Causeway Visitor Centre have cafés (the latter is only for those with a ticket). The town of Bushmills has a handful of places for an easy lunch. Near Dunseverick Castle, **$ Bothy** is a coffee house with good breakfast and lunch offerings in a relaxing cabin-like space (Mon-Sat 9:00-17:00, closed Sun, on the main road a 10-minute drive east of Giant's Causeway, +44 28 2073 2311, www.bothycoffee.com).

Sights on the Antrim Coast

▲▲Giant's Causeway

This five-mile-long stretch of coastline is famous for its bizarre basalt columns. The shore is covered with largely hexagonal pillars that stick up at various heights. It's as if the earth were offering God a choice of 37,000 six-sided cigarettes.

Geologists claim the Giant's Causeway was formed by volcanic eruptions more than 60 million years ago. As the surface of the lava flow quickly cooled, it contracted and crystallized into columns (resembling the caked mud at the bottom of a dried-up lakebed, but with far deeper cracks). As the rock later settled and eroded, the columns broke off into the many stair-like steps that now honeycomb the Antrim Coast.

Of course, in actuality, the Giant's Causeway was made by a giant Ulster warrior named Finn MacCool who knew of a rival giant living across the water in Scotland. Finn built a stone bridge over to Scotland to spy on his rival and found out that the Scottish giant was much bigger. Finn retreated to Ireland and had his wife dress him as a sleeping infant, just in time for the rival giant

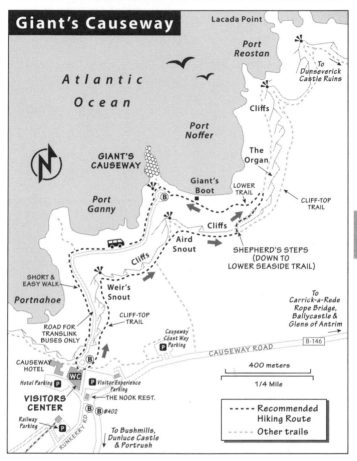

to come across the causeway to spy on Finn. The rival, shocked at the infant's size, fled back to Scotland in terror of whomever had sired this giant baby. Breathing a sigh of relief, Finn tore off the baby clothes and prudently knocked down the bridge. Today, proof of this encounter exists in the geologic formation that still extends undersea and surfaces in Scotland (at the island of Staffa).

Orientation to the Giant's Causeway

You have two choices for visiting the causeway: on your own, or with a Visitor Experience ticket.

Cost and Hours: It's free to visit the Giant's Causeway, and the coastline is open and accessible to visitors from dawn till dusk. It's £13 for a Visitor Experience timed-entry ticket, which includes reserved premium parking, your choice of an audioguide or one-hour guided walk to the causeway, and entry to the visitors center, which has a small exhibit, plus a shop and café (visitors center open

Antrim Coast

Atlantic

A N T R I M

3 Kilometers

3 Miles

Skerries Islands

Cliffs

Giant's
Causeway
See detail map

VISITORS
CENTER

B-146

A-2

Portrush
See detail map

DUNLUCE
CASTLE

GOLF
COURSE

A-2

Bushmills

BUSHMILLS
DISTILERY

Portstewart

A-2

A-29

CASTLECAT ROAD

B-62

To
Derry

A-2

B-67

Derrykeighan

Coleraine

Ballybogey

B-66

River Bann

To
Derry

A-29

A-26

B-66

A-37

To Belfast

To Ballymoney & Belfast

daily 9:00-17:00, off-season 10:00-16:00, +44 28 2073 1855, www.
nationaltrust.org.uk/giantscauseway). In summer, prebooking is
strongly recommended for the Visitor Experience (bookings open
up four weeks in advance).

When to Go: If visiting on your own, it's best to go first thing
in the morning or early evening, as summer days are long, crowds
are fewer, and parking is easier. If you plan to get a Visitor Experience ticket, try to book one of the first or last time slots, as the
majority of big bus tours generally roll through between 11:00 and
15:30.

Getting There: Without a car, you can take the Rambler bus
or a taxi (see "Getting Around the Antrim Coast," earlier). Drivers
will find parking to be a challenge in peak season. Those with a
Visitor Experience ticket have guaranteed parking next to the visitors center. Otherwise, try the Causeway Coast Way lot (£5) or the
Railway lot (£9; for locations, see the Giant's Causeway map in this

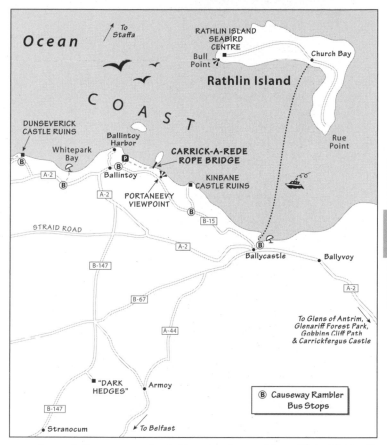

Ocean

To Staffa

COAST

RATHLIN ISLAND
SEABIRD
CENTRE

Bull
Point

Church Bay

Rathlin Island

Rue
Point

DUNSEVERICK
CASTLE RUINS

Ballintoy
Harbor

**CARRICK-A-REDE
ROPE BRIDGE**

Whitepark
Bay

Ballintoy

KINBANE
CASTLE RUINS

A-2

A-2

PORTANEEVY
VIEWPOINT

B-15

STRAID ROAD

A-2

Ballycastle

Ballyvoy

A-2

B-147

B-67

To Glens of Antrim,
Glenariff Forest Park,
Gobbins Cliff Path
& Carrickfergus Castle

A-44

"DARK
HEDGES"

Armoy

Ⓑ Causeway Rambler
Bus Stops

B-147

Stranocum

To Belfast

PORTRUSH & ANTRIM COAST

chapter). Sometimes the field across the road from Finn McCool's Hostel opens for parking.

Visiting the Causeway

If you have a Visitor Experience ticket, start in the **Giant's Causeway Visitor Centre.** It's filled with interactive exhibits giving a worthwhile history of the Giant's Causeway, with a regional overview. On the far wall near the entrance, check out the interesting three-minute video showing the evolution of the causeway from molten lava to the geometric, geologic wonderland of today. The

large 3-D model of the causeway offers a bird's-eye view of the region.

The **causeway** itself is the highlight of the entire coast. Whether doing the Visitor Experience or hiking on your own, you have several options for visiting the causeway. Note that the trail colors mentioned below correspond to the ones displayed on maps at the sight.

Short and Easy Walk (or Bus Ride): The most direct and easy route to the causeway is via the blue trail, a gentle one-mile out-and-back walk along a paved road (downhill on the way there, uphill coming back). If you don't want to walk, you can take a **Translink bus** (4/hour, £1 each way), which zips tourists from the visitors center down the same road to the causeway. If you have the Visitor Experience ticket, you can join a guided tour or listen to the audioguide as you walk along this road. Many choose to walk down and then take the bus back up.

Just below the bus stop is a fine place to explore the uneven, wave-splashed rock terraces. Look for "wishing coins"—rusted and bent—that have been jammed into the cracks of rock just behind the turnaround (where the trail passes through a notch in the 20-foot-high rock wall).

Mid-Level Loop Hike: For a longer hike and a more varied dose of causeway views, consider a loop hike connecting the red trail (along the cliffs, then down to the causeway) and back up along the blue trail (about two miles).

Starting at the visitors center, find the cliff-top path (red trail). Follow it uphill 10 minutes to Weir's Snout, the great fence-protected precipice viewpoint. Then hike 15 level minutes farther to reach the Shepherd's Steps. Head down the steep (and slippery-when-wet) stairs that switchback toward the water. At the T-junction, go 100 yards right, to the towering basaltic pipes of the Organ. (You can detour another 500 yards east around the headland, but the trail dead-ends there.) Now retrace your steps west on the trail (don't go up the steps again), continuing down to the tidal zone, where the Giant's Boot (6-foot boulder, on the right) provides some photo fun. Another 100 yards farther is the dramatic point where the causeway meets the sea. Just beyond that, at the turnaround, is the road back up to the visitors center (blue trail); you can walk up or take the bus (described earlier).

Longer Hike (One-Way): Hardy hikers can walk the one-way five-mile route (yellow trail) that runs along a scenic section of the causeway coast, starting at the meager ruins of Dunseverick Castle (east of Giant's Causeway on B-146) and ending at the Giant's Causeway Visitor Centre. Expect undulating grass and gravel paths (no WCs, no shelter from bad weather). Note that occasional rock falls and slides can close this trail (ask first at Portrush TI or call ahead to visitors center).

With a Guide: One way to do this hike is to join the guided **Clifftop Experience.** Hikers meet their guide at the Giant's Causeway Visitors Centre and bus to the Dunseverick trailhead (£39, includes parking and visitors center access, daily at 12:15, must book online by 16:00 a day ahead, allow 4 hours, no kids under 12, +44 78 3770 3643, www.awayaweewalk.com).

On Your Own: Since the trails here are all a public right-of-way, you are welcome to hike on your own. A good plan is to take the Causeway Rambler bus (see "Getting Around the Antrim Coast," earlier) or a taxi from Portrush to Dunseverick Castle and the trailhead (there's also limited parking at the Dunseverick Castle trailhead). From the castle, hike west, following the cliff-hugging contours of Benbane Head back to the visitors center. You'll generally have a fence on your left and the cliff on the right, so there's little doubt about the route. When you reach the visitors center, call a taxi or ride the Rambler bus back to your car or hotel (check bus schedules ahead of time at www.translink.co.uk). For more info on hiking the route, see VisitCausewayCoastandGlens. com and search for "North Antrim Cliff Path."

▲▲Old Bushmills Distillery

Bushmills claims to be the world's oldest distillery. Though King James I (of Bible translation fame) only granted Bushmills its license to distill "Aqua Vitae" in 1608, whiskey has been made here since the 13th century. Distillery tours waft you through the process, making it clear that Irish whiskey is triple distilled—and therefore smoother than Scotch whisky (distilled merely twice).

Cost and Hours: Book ahead online for one-hour guided tour (£10, includes tasting); tours run every 30 or 60 minutes Mon-Sat from 10:00 until 15:00 or 16:00 (last tour), Sun from 12:00; tours are limited to 16-18 people and can fill up far in advance; if tours are sold out, keep checking, as additional tours are sometimes added last-minute; note that for about a week in July, the distillery machinery is shut down for annual maintenance (though tours still run); cafeteria, bar, and shop open to all visitors; +44 28 2073 3218, www.bushmills.com.

Visiting the Distillery: Bushmills is made of only three in-

For *Game of Thrones* Fans

Even if you don't give a bloody Stark about the *Game of Thrones* TV saga, you'll notice references to it as you travel around Northern Ireland. Much of the series was filmed here, both on location and in the Titanic Quarter studio in Belfast. An average visit to the Antrim Coast is a traipse through the set: Dragonstone, the Stormlands, and the Iron Islands were brought to life along the same route that travelers use to see Dunluce Castle and Carrick-a-Rede Rope Bridge. For those who are truly interested in the approach of a very long winter, there are several options: both McComb's (www.mccombscoaches.com; see page 65) and Game of Thrones Tours (www.gameofthronestours.com) run day tours from Belfast or Derry to various spots in the seven kingdoms.

With a car, use the Game of Thrones pages at DiscoverNorthernIreland.com to find filming locations. Without leaving County Antrim, you can visit Ballintoy Harbour (Stormlands), Larrybane (Iron Islands), Murlough Bay (Storm's End), and the Dark Hedges (King's Road) with no more than an hour's driving time. Just avoid any reenactments, as the nearest major hospital that treats dragon burns is in Belfast.

gredients: malted barley, water, and yeast. Tours start with the mash pit, which is filled with a porridge that eventually becomes whiskey. (The leftovers of that porridge are fed to the county's particularly happy cows.) Next you'll see some impressive equipment, including giant washbacks—where yeast is added to the mixture to induce fermentation, producing alcohol—and copper pot stills, where distillation increases the alcohol content.

In the casking factory, you'll see a huge room full of whiskey aging in oak casks—casks already used to make bourbon, sherry, and port. Whiskey picks up its color and personality from this wood (which breathes and has an effective life of 30 years). Bushmills shapes the flavor of its whiskey by carefully finessing the aging process—often in a mix of these casks.

To see the distillery at its lively best, visit when the workers are staffing the machinery—Monday morning through Friday noon. The finale, of course, is the opportunity for a sip in the 1608 Bar—the former malt barn. Visitors get a single glass of their choice. Those who don't want straight-up whiskey can ask for a cocktail (such as a cinnamon-and-cloves hot toddy) or a nonalcoholic beverage.

Shoppers: The distillery cannot ship purchases.

Nearby: The distillery is just outside of **Bushmills town,** with a few places to eat, groceries, gas, and other services along the main drag. If you wander into the side streets, you'll see some red, white, and blue flags and other signs of Unionist loyalty.

▲▲Carrick-a-Rede Rope Bridge

For 200 years, using just wooden planks, rope, and wire, fishermen strung a narrow, 90-foot-high bridge across a 65-foot-wide chasm between the mainland and the tiny island of Carrick-a-Rede. Today, the bridge (while not the original version) gives access to the sea stack where salmon nets were set during summer months to catch the fish turning and hugging the coast's corner. (With the

salmon run depleted, the fishery shut down in 2002.) A pleasant, 30-minute, one-mile walk from the parking lot takes you down to the rope bridge. Cross over to the island for fine views and great seabird-watching, especially during nesting season. Even if you don't have a ticket to cross, the walk to the bridge is worthwhile, as it's easy and provides fine views of the coastline and bridge.

Cost and Hours: £13 to cross the bridge—must book timed-entry ticket online in advance, £5 to park in the lot and walk the trail to the bridge; bridge open daily 9:30-16:30, parking lot daily 9:00-18:00, closed in winter; coffee shop and WCs near the parking lot, +44 28 2076 9839, www.nationaltrust.org.uk/carrick-a-rede. Note that the bridge can close in windy weather.

Nearby Viewpoint: If you have a car and a picnic lunch, don't miss the terrific coastal scenic rest area one mile steeply uphill and east of Carrick-a-Rede (on B-15 to Ballycastle). This grassy area offers one of the best picnic views in Northern Ireland (tables but no WCs). Feast on bird's-eye views of the rope bridge, nearby Rathlin Island, and the not-so-distant Island of Mull in Scotland.

▲Dunluce Castle

These romantic ruins, perched dramatically on the edge of a rocky headland, are a testimony to this region's turbulent past. During the Middle Ages, the castle was a prized fortification. But on a stormy night in 1639, dinner was interrupted as half of the kitchen fell into the sea, taking the servants with it. That was the last straw for the lady of the castle. The countess of

Antrim packed up and moved inland, and the castle began its slow submission to the forces of nature.

Cost and Hours: £6, daily 9:30-17:00, until 16:00 in winter, +44 28 2073 1938.

Visiting the Castle: While it's one of the largest castles in Northern Ireland and is beautifully situated, there's precious little left to see among Dunluce's broken walls. Look for distinctively hexagonal stones embedded in the castle walls, plucked straight from the unique pillars of rock making up the nearby Giant's Causeway.

Before entering, catch the eight-minute video about the history of the castle (across from the ticket desk). From there, follow the stops laid out on the map that comes with your admission. The ruins themselves are dotted with plaques that show interesting artists' renditions of how the place would have looked 400 years ago.

There were primitive fortifications here hundreds of years before the castle was built. But the 16th century saw the biggest expansion of the castle, financed by treasure salvaged from a shipwreck. In 1588, the Spanish Armada's *Girona*—overloaded with sailors and the valuables of three abandoned sister ships—sank on her way home after the aborted mission against England. More than 1,300 drowned, and only five survivors washed ashore. The shipwreck was more fully excavated in 1967, and a bounty of golden odds and silver ends wound up in Belfast's Ulster Museum.

Rathlin Island

The only inhabited island off the coast of Northern Ireland, Rathlin is a quiet haven for hikers, birdwatchers, and seal spotters.

Less than seven miles from end to end, this L-shaped island is reachable by ferry from the town of Ballycastle. Plan on spending about a half-day for your visit.

Getting There: The Rathlin Island passenger-only ferry departs from Ballycastle, just east of Carrick-a-Rede. In peak season, it runs about hourly 8:00-18:00 with a midday break—check the schedule online. It's smart to book in advance for July-Aug. Spots can be booked online up to 24 hours in advance; after that you must book through the office—either in person or by phone (£12 round-trip per passenger, 25 minutes by fast ferry, 40 minutes by cargo ferry, also runs in winter about every 2 hours; +44 28 2076 9299, www.rathlinballycastleferry.com).

Drivers can park in Ballycastle (only special-permit holders can take a car onto the ferry). A taxi from Portrush to Ballycastle runs about £35 one-way. Bus service from Portrush to Ballycastle is available but hard to time with the ferry (for bus schedule, check the journey planner at www.translink.co.uk).

Visiting Rathlin Island

Rathlin's population of 110 islanders clusters around the ferry dock at Church Bay. Here you'll find the **Rathlin Boathouse Visitor Centre,** which operates as the island's TI (daily 10:00-17:00, closed in winter, on the bay 100 yards east of the ferry dock, +44 28 2076 0054). There are also some shops and a few places to eat.

Rathlin Island Seabird Centre: This center, at the west end of the island, gives visitors viewing access to Northern Ireland's largest colony of seabirds, including puffins, razorbills, and guillemots (birdwatching season runs about mid-April to early August). A shuttle bus (£5 round-trip) meets arriving ferries and drives visitors to the center (or you can walk or bike—see below). Entry to the Seabird Centre includes a tour of its unique lighthouse, extending down the cliff with its beacon at the bottom. It's upside-down because the coast guard wants the light visible only from a certain distance out to sea. The bird observation terrace at the center (next to the lighthouse) overlooks one of the most dramatic coastal views in Ireland—a sheer drop of more than 300 feet to craggy sea stacks just offshore that are draped with thousands of seabirds (£5, daily mid-April-mid-Sept 9:30-17:00, last entry one hour before closing, closed off-season, www.rspb.org.uk/reserves-and-events/reserves-a-z/rathlin-island).

Hiking and Biking: With time, you can hike or bike to the Seabird Centre, or around the island (there are several walking trails; look them up at www.walkni.com/causeway-coast-glens-destination). **Rathlin Cycle Hire** rents bikes from near the ferry dock (must prebook, +44 28 2076 3954). Or you can join a walking tour; check the offerings from **Rathlin Walking Tours** (www.rathlinwalkingtours.com) or **Nine Glens,** which also offers paddleboarding on Rathlin Island (www.nineglensadventuretours.co.uk).

Rathlin has seen its fair share of history. Flint ax heads were quarried here in Neolithic times. The island was one of the first in Ireland to be raided by Vikings, in 795. Robert the Bruce hid out from English pursuers on Rathlin in the early 1300s (see "The Scottish Connection" sidebar, earlier). In the late 1500s, local warlord Sorely Boy MacDonnell stashed his extended family on Rathlin and waited on the mainland at Dunluce Castle to face his English enemies...only to watch in horror as they headed for the island instead to massacre his loved ones. And in 1917, a WWI U-boat sank the British cruiser HMS *Drake* in Church Bay. The wreck is now a popular scuba-dive destination, 60 feet below the surface.

▲Antrim Mountains and Glens

Not particularly high (never more than 1,500 feet), the Antrim Mountains are cut by a series of large glens—narrow valleys—running northeast to the sea. Glenariff, with its waterfalls—especially the Mare's Tail—is the most beautiful of the nine glens (described next). Travelers going by car can take a pleasant drive from Portrush to Belfast, sticking to the (more scenic but less direct) A-2 road that stays near the coast and takes in parts of all the Glens of Antrim.

Glenariff Forest Park: This ▲ park offers scenic picnic spots and lush hiking trails as well as a cozy tea shop. The parking lot alone has a lovely view down the glen to the sea. You'll find more spectacular scenery on the two-mile waterfall walkway trail along the river gorge, while an easygoing half-mile stroll on the viewpoint trail via the ornamental gardens also provides lovely views (£5 parking, daily 8:00-dusk, trail map available at café onsite, +44 28 7034 0870, www.nidirect.gov.uk).

Getting There: The entry is off A-43 (via A-26; eight miles south of Cushendall, follow signs).

Nearby: Continue along the A-2 scenic coastal route and take a short jog up to Cushendall, where there's a nice beach for a picnic, or just head south on A-2 toward the Gobbins Cliff Path and the castle at Carrickfergus (see listings in the Belfast chapter).

BELFAST

Northern Ireland's capital city is best known for its role in the Troubles, and as the birthplace of the *Titanic* (and many other ships that didn't sink).

Today the historic Titanic Quarter symbolizes the rise of Belfast. The city is bristling with cranes and busy with tourists. It's hard to believe that the bright and bustling pedestrian center was once a subdued, traffic-free security zone. These days, while Catholics and Protestants still generally live and study in segregated zones, they are totally integrated where they work—and they all root for the Belfast Giants ice hockey team. Aggressive sectarian murals are slowly being repainted with scenes celebrating heritage pride... less carnage, more culture. It feels like a new morning in Belfast.

PLANNING YOUR TIME

If you're staying in Dublin and not planning on visiting Belfast, reconsider. A long day trip from Dublin to Belfast is one of the most interesting days you could have anywhere in Ireland, and it's just a two-hour train ride away (about €32 for tickets).

Day Trip from Dublin

This ambitious plan works on any day but Sunday, when trains don't run as early or late:

7:35	Catch the train from Dublin's Connolly Station
9:45	Arrive at Belfast's Lanyon Place/Central Station
10:00	Visit City Hall and browse the pedestrian zone
12:00	Lunch
13:00	Tour the sectarian neighborhoods in West Belfast

BELFAST

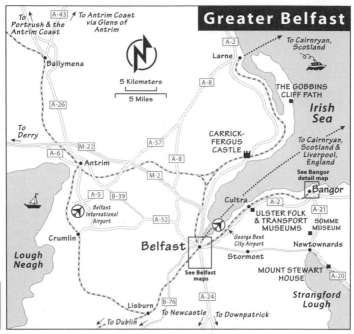

15:00   Visit the Titanic Belfast Museum (after midday crowds subside)
17:30   Dinner in the Titanic Quarter or Cathedral Quarter
20:05   Catch the train back to Dublin

With More Time

If you're circling Ireland by car, Belfast can easily fill two days of sightseeing. On the first day, follow my day-trip itinerary. On the second day, consider side-tripping to sights outside of town, such as the Ulster Folk Museum, Ulster Transport Museum, and/or Carrickfergus Castle.

Orientation to Belfast

Belfast is flat and spread out. Restaurants and live music venues are all within walking distance of the town center. When planning, think of Belfast as having four sightseeing zones:

Central Belfast: The perfectly walkable city center has a dozen or so mostly minor sights that are never crowded and often free. Sights include City Hall on Donegall Square, pedestrian shopping areas, and the Cathedral Quarter with its lively night scene.

West Belfast: The working-class, sectarian neighborhoods along Falls Road and Shankill Road, while walkable, are much more interesting with a taxi tour.

Titanic Quarter: The northeast bank of the River Lagan is dominated by the Titanic Belfast Museum, but there's much more here, including a wonderful riverside stroll with a string of sightseeing stops along the way.

South Belfast: This neighborhood is home to the fine Ulster Museum and Botanic Gardens. It's also where you'll find more cozy B&B guesthouses, rather than just chain hotels.

TOURIST INFORMATION

The modern TI (look for *Visit Belfast* sign) faces City Hall and has a courteous staff, a Translink bus and rail desk, and baggage storage (Mon-Sat 9:00-17:30, June-Sept until 19:00, Sun 11:00-16:00 year-round; 9 Donegall Square North, +44 28 9024 6609, http://visitbelfast.com). Pick up a free copy of *Visit Belfast,* which lists all the sightseeing and evening entertainment options.

ARRIVAL IN BELFAST

By Train: Arriving at Belfast's Lanyon Place/Central Station, it's a 15-minute **walk** to City Hall/Donegall Square in the city center.

By **bus,** take the Glider #G1, which goes to City Hall (runs every 8 minutes or so, free with any train or bus ticket, the stop is out the station and 25 yards to the right). If staying in South Belfast, you can ride the #G1 into the center, then from Donegall Square East, catch a #8 bus.

To take a **taxi,** go downstairs and call for one on the freephone next to the pickup point. Allow about £6-8 for a taxi to Donegall Square or the Titanic Belfast Museum; £10-12 to my accommodation listings south of the university.

Slower trains arc through the city, stopping at several downtown stations, including Great Victoria Street Station (most central, near Donegall Square and most hotels) and Botanic Station (close to the university, Botanic Gardens, and some recommended lodgings). It's easy and cheap to connect stations by train (£1.70).

If day-tripping into Belfast from Bangor, use the station closest to your targeted sights. Note that trains cost the same from Bangor to all three Belfast stations (Lanyon Place/Central, Great Victoria Street, and Botanic).

By Car: Driving in Belfast is a pain. Avoid it if possible. Street parking in the city center is geared for short stops (use pay-and-dis-

Belfast's Troubled History

Seventeenth-century Belfast grew from being a village where rope, nets, and sailcloth were made to an emerging port with shipbuilding interests. The city built many of the world's biggest and finest ships. And when the American Civil War shut down the US cotton industry, the linen mills of Belfast were beneficiaries. In fact Belfast became known as "Linen-opolis."

The Industrial Revolution took root in Belfast with a vengeance. While the rest of Ireland remained rural and agricultural, Belfast earned another nickname, "Old Smoke," during the time when many of the brick buildings that you'll see today were built.

The year 1888 marked the birth of modern Belfast. After Queen Victoria granted Belfast city status, it boomed. The population (only 20,000 in 1800) reached 350,000 by 1900. And its citizens built Belfast's centerpiece—its grand City Hall.

Belfast was also busy building ships, from transoceanic liners like the ill-fated *Titanic* to naval vessels during the world wars. (Belfast's famous shipyards were strategic enough to be the target of four German Luftwaffe bombing raids in World War II.) Two huge, mustard-colored, rectangular gantry cranes (built in the 1970s, and once the biggest in the world, nicknamed Samson and Goliath) stand like idle giants over the shipyards—a reminder of Belfast's shipbuilding might.

Of course, the sectarian Troubles ravaged Belfast along with the rest of Northern Ireland from 1969 to 1998—a time when downtown Belfast was ringed with security checks and nearly shut down at night. There was almost no tourism for decades (and only a few pubs downtown). Thankfully, at the beginning of the 21st century, the peace process began to take root, and investments from south of the border—the Republic of Ireland—injected new life into the dejected shipyards where the *Titanic* was built.

Still, it's a fragile peace. Hateful bonfires, built a month before they're set ablaze, still scorch the pavement in working-class Protestant neighborhoods each July. Pubs with security gates are reminders that the island is still split—and 900,000 Protestant Unionists in the north prefer it that way.

play machines, most streets are £1.40/hour, one-hour maximum, Mon-Sat 8:00-18:00, free in evenings and on Sun).

By Plane: For information on Belfast's airports, see the "Belfast Connections" section on page 101.

HELPFUL HINTS

Belfast Visitor Pass: This pass combines sightseeing discounts with iLink smartcards for free bus, rail, and tram rides within the Belfast Visitor Pass Zone (downtown Belfast as far out as the Ulster Folk Museum and Ulster Transport Museum in Cultra, but not as far as Carrickfergus or Bangor). It also includes discounts for the Titanic Belfast Museum (£3 off) and some tours (see list of discounts on Visitor Pass page of VisitBelfast.com). Buy it at the TI, any train station, either airport, Europa Bus station, or online (1-day pass-£6, 2 consecutive days-£11, 3 days-£14.50, +44 28 9066 6630, www. translink.co.uk/belfast-visitor-pass).

Market: On Friday, Saturday, and Sunday, the Victorian confines of **St. George's Market** are a commotion of commerce and a people-watching delight (see page 74).

Shopping Mall: Victoria Square is a glitzy American-style mall where you can find whatever you need (1 Victoria Square, three blocks east of City Hall, www.victoriasquare.com).

Laundry: Globe Launderers has both self-serve and drop-off service (Mon-Fri 8:00-17:00, Sat from 9:00, Sun 12:00-16:00, 39 Botanic Avenue, +44 28 9024 3956). **Whistle Cleaners** is handy to hotels south of the university (drop-off service, Mon-Sat 9:00-17:00, closed Sun, 160 Lisburn Road, at intersection with Eglantine Avenue, +44 28 9038 1297). For locations, see the map on page 90.

Bike Rental: Belfast City Bikes rents bikes of all types, from fancy electric (£50/day) to three-speed cruisers (£15/day). It's located at Norm's Bikes, near the Cathedral Quarter (Unit 18 Smithfield Marketplace, Winetavern Street). They also offer bike tours (for contact info, see their listing later, under "Tours in Belfast").

GETTING AROUND BELFAST

If you line up your sightseeing logically, you can do most of this flat city on foot. But for more far-flung sights, the train, bus, or tram can be useful. If you plan to use public transit, consider the Belfast Visitor Pass (see "Helpful Hints," earlier).

By Train, Bus, or Glider Bus: Translink operates Belfast's system of trains, buses, and Glider buses (+44 28 9066 6630, www. translink.co.uk).

At any **train** station, ask about iLink smartcards, which cover one day of unlimited train, Glider, and bus travel. The Zone 1 card (£5) covers the city center, Cultra (Ulster Folk Museum and Transport Museum), and George Best Belfast City Airport. The handy Zone 2 card (£10) adds Bangor and Carrickfergus Castle. The Zone 3 card (£13.50) is only useful for reaching Belfast's distant international airport. Zone 4 (£16.50) gets you anywhere in Northern Ireland, including Portrush and Derry. For those lingering in the north, one-week cards offer even better deals. Without a pass, if you're traveling from Belfast to only one destination—Carrick-

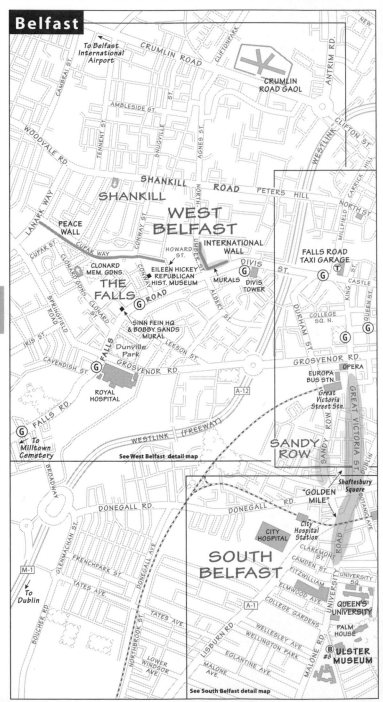

Belfast

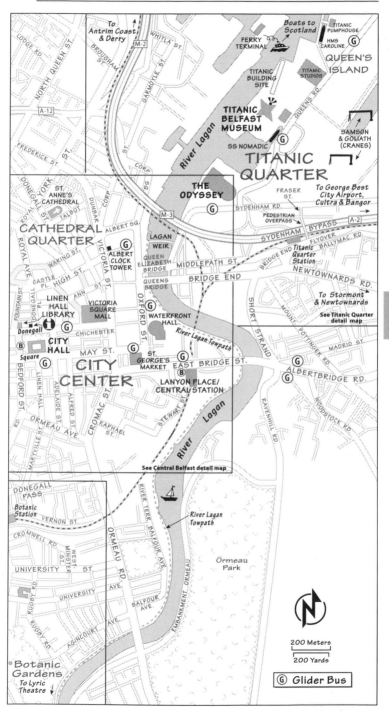

BELFAST

200 Meters
200 Yards

Ⓖ Glider Bus

fergus Castle, Cultra, or Bangor—a "day return" ticket is cheaper than two one-way tickets.

Pink-and-white city **buses** go from Donegall Square East to Malone Road and my recommended accommodations (any #8 bus, 2-4/hour, covered by iLink smartcards, otherwise £2.10, £4.20 all-day pass).

The slick rapid-transit **Glider bus** (described as a "tram on wheels") opened in 2018 and has two lines. The #G1 line connects East and West Belfast (every 8 minutes Mon-Fri, less frequent Sat-Sun), while the #G2 goes from the city center to the Titanic-area sights (2-4/hour). At each Glider stop you'll find route maps, a board showing wait times, and ticket machines (buy ticket before you board, credit cards OK). Rides cost £1.60 for most tourist routes (more if traveling outside the city center, covered by iLink smartcards).

By Taxi: Taxis are reasonable and easy. You can flag one down, ask your restaurant or hotel to call one for you, or order one yourself through either **Value Cabs** (+44 28 9080 9080) or **fonaCAB** (+44 28 9033 3333). Both companies have mobile apps that make it easy to summon a ride. (Note that while Uber operates here, it isn't as common, and your fare will still be metered). If you're going up Falls Road, ride a shared cab (described later, under "Touring the Sectarian Neighborhoods").

Tours in Belfast

Beyond the tours listed below, I highly recommend visiting the **sectarian neighborhoods** in West Belfast on a taxi or walking tour (see the "Touring the Sectarian Neighborhoods" listing later, under "Sights in Belfast").

ON FOOT

Belfast's history is more interesting than its actual sights (and its people are really fun to get to know). A guided walk makes a lot of sense here. In fact, you could take several guided walks, as each one would be filled with entertaining insights on different angles of the city (and tours are relatively cheap).

Walking Tours

Free tours are actually "pay what you think it's worth" tours, led by locals who spin a good yarn while sharing the basics of the city. These tours take a couple hours and leave from in front of City Hall, across from the TI (daily in season at 11:00 and 14:30, just show up, www.belfastfreewalkingtour.com).

Experience Belfast Tours runs a 2.5-hour "Troubles" tour that includes City Hall, the Cathedral Quarter, and the Linen Hall

Library, plus the River Lagan and Belfast's city center murals (£18, daily at 10:00, meets in front of the City Hall main gate facing Donegall Square North—look for green and white umbrella, +44 77 7164 0746, https://experiencebelfast.com).

Belfast Hidden Tours offers several walking tours. Find out about current offerings online or over the phone (+44 79 7189 5746, www.belfasthiddentours.com).

Food Tours

Taste & Tour offers a palate-pleasing array of tours covering food, beer, and whiskey. Tours are generally small, include five stops, and are lots of fun. The general "Belfast Food Tour" runs Friday and Saturday only and books up well in advance (£62, 3-4 hours, +44 28 9045 7723, www.tasteandtour.co.uk).

Local Guides

Dee Morgan is smart and delightful. She grew up on Falls Road and can tailor your tour to history, food, politics, or music (£180/half-day, info@deetoursireland.com).

Susie Millar is a sharp former BBC TV reporter with family connections to the *Titanic* tragedy. She can also take you farther afield by car (yours or hers, 3-hour tour-£30/person, +44 78 5271 6655, www.titanictours-belfast.co.uk, info@titanictours-belfast.co.uk).

Lynn Corken is another knowledgeable and flexible Jill-of-all-guiding trades, with a passion for her hometown, politics, history, and Van Morrison (on foot or with her car, £100/half-day, £200/day, +44 77 7910 2448, lynncorken@hotmail.co.uk).

Lolly Spence, a former BBC producer, offers walking, hiking, cycling, and driving tours specializing in C. S. Lewis, *Game of Thrones*, Ulster-Scots, and local history (£150/half-day, £250/full day, +44 79 0098 8886, lspence@hiddenulstertours.com).

ON WHEELS
▲Hop-On, Hop-Off Bus Tours

Two different hop-on, hop-off buses loop around Belfast, but tickets can be used interchangeably, so you can ride any open-top bus.

City Sightseeing offers the best quick introduction to the city's political and social history. Their open-top, double-decker buses link major sights and landmarks, including the Catholic and Protestant working-class neighborhoods, the Stor-

Belfast at a Glance

▲▲▲**Titanic Belfast Museum** Excellent high-tech exhibit covering the famously infamous ship and local shipbuilding, in a stunning structure on the site where the *Titanic* was built. **Hours:** Daily 9:00-18:00, June-Aug until 19:00, Oct-March 10:00-17:00. See page 86.

▲▲▲**Sectarian Neighborhoods** Ride with local cabbies or join a tour (walking or taxi) through West Belfast's Falls Road and Shankill Road neighborhoods, listening to personal perspectives on the slowly fading Troubles. See page 74.

▲▲**City Hall** Central Belfast's polished and majestic celebration of Victorian-era pride built with industrial wealth. **Hours:** Mon-Fri 9:30-17:00, closed Sat-Sun. See page 66.

▲▲**Live Music** For the cost of a beer, connect with Belfast's culture, people, and music in a pub. **Hours:** Nightly after 21:30. See page 95.

▲**HMS *Caroline*** WWI battleship that looks just like it did at the Battle of Jutland in 1916. **Hours:** Daily 10:00-17:00. See page 88.

▲**St. George's Market** Thriving scene filling a huge Victorian market hall with artisans, junk dealers, street food, and fun. **Hours:** Fri-Sun 9:00-14:00 or 15:00. See page 74.

▲**Crumlin Road Gaol** Victorian-era jail with displays and re-creations of prison life. **Hours:** Daily 10:30-17:00, Fri-Sat until 18:30 in summer. See page 78.

▲**Ulster Museum** Mixed bag of local artifacts, natural history, and coverage of political events; a good rainy-day option near

mont Parliament building, Titanic Belfast Museum, and the sights near Queens University (Ulster Museum and Botanic Gardens), with commentary on political murals and places of interest. The route, which covers 19 stops in about 70 minutes, departs from Donegall Square West, near City Hall—but you can hop on anywhere (£18/24 hours, £23/48 hours, book online or pay on bus with cash or card, runs every 30 minutes, daily 10:00-16:00, +44 28 9032 1321, http://belfastcitysightseeing.com).

City Tours offers a route with 19 stops that takes 75-90 minutes. It starts at Donegall Square West, then veers westward to take in Falls and Shankill roads (£23/24 hours, £29/48 hours, family tickets available, book online or pay cash on bus, departs

Queen's University. **Hours:** Tue-Sun 10:00-17:00, closed Mon. See page 89.

▲**Botanic Gardens** Belfast's best green space, featuring the Palm House loaded with delicate tropical vegetation. **Hours:** Gardens daily 8:00 until dusk; shorter hours for Palm House and Tropical Ravine. See page 90.

Near Belfast
▲▲**Ulster Folk Museum and Ulster Transport Museum** A glimpse into Northern Ireland's hardworking heritage, split between a charming re-creation of past rural life and halls of vehicular innovation (8 miles east of Belfast). **Hours:** Tue-Sun 10:00-17:00; Oct-Feb Tue-Fri 10:00-16:00, Sat-Sun from 11:00; closed Mon year-round. See page 92.

▲**Carrickfergus Castle** Northern Ireland's first and most important fortified refuge for invading 12th-century Normans (14 miles northeast of Belfast). **Hours:** Tue-Sun 9:30-17:00, closed Mon. See page 93.

▲**The Gobbins Cliff Path** Rugged, unique, wave-splashed hiking trail cut into coastal rock, accessible by guided tour (34 miles northeast of Belfast). **Hours:** Visitors center daily 8:30-17:00, guided hikes about hourly in good weather. See page 94.

Near Bangor
▲**Mount Stewart House** Fine 18th-century manor house displaying ruling-class affluence, surrounded by lush and calming gardens (18 miles east of Belfast). **Hours:** Daily 11:00-17:00, closed Nov-Feb. See page 105.

BELFAST

every 30-45 minutes, daily 10:00-16:00, +44 28 9032 1912, www. citytoursbelfast.com).

Countryside Bus Tours
McComb's offers several big-bus tours, day-tripping out of Belfast to distant points. Their "Giant's Causeway Tour" visits Carrickfergus Castle (photo stop), the Giant's Causeway, and Dunluce Castle (photo stop). Their "*Game of Thrones* Tour" visits many of the sites where the hit TV series was filmed (either tour: £25/person, daily, pickup at 8:30 from in front of the Europa Hotel, return by 17:30, book ahead by phone or online, +44 28 9031 5333, www. mccombscoaches.com, info@mccombscoaches.com).

Bike Tours

Belfast City Bikes offers a three-hour city tour that covers the Cathedral Quarter, Titanic Quarter, Queen's University area, and city center (£30/person, daily at 10:00 in summer, Thu-Sun only in off-season). They also offer a "Bike and Brew" tour that cycles out to Hilden Brewery (about 12.5 miles) for lunch and beer sampling; it's your choice to ride or take the train back to the city (£50, includes lunch, Thu-Sun at 10:00, 4 hours, for either tour reserve ahead via phone or email, +44 77 8049 6969, www.belfastcitybiketours.com, info@belfastcitybiketours.com).

Sights in Belfast

CENTRAL BELFAST

The sights of central Belfast are mostly minor but fun to check out. Nearly all are within a 10-minute walk of City Hall.

Donegall Square and Nearby
▲▲City Hall

This grand structure's 173-foot-tall copper dome dominates Donegall Square at the center of town. Built between 1898 and 1906, with its statue of Queen Victoria scowling

down Belfast's main drag and the Neoclassical dome looming behind her, City Hall is a stirring sight. The worthwhile 16-room visitor exhibit fills the ground floor, covering the history of the building and local government, language, culture, industry, and wars and turmoil. The Belfast Hall of Fame features local celebrities, from scientists and writers to sports stars and musicians.

Cost and Hours: Exhibit is free, open Mon-Fri 9:30-17:00, closed Sat-Sun, last entry one hour before closing, may open weekends in summer—check online, ask about audioguide, recommended Bobbin coffee shop on ground floor, +44 28 9032 0202, www.belfastcity.gov.uk/cityhall. They sometimes run guided tours of the building—check online for schedule and to book a spot.

Linen Hall Library

Across the street from City Hall, the 200-year-old Linen Hall Library welcomes guests (notice the red hand above the front door facing Donegall Square North; for more on its meaning, see the sidebar on page 91). Described as "Ulster's attic," the library takes pride in being a neutral space for anyone trying to make sense of the sectarian conflict. To view a historical collection of political posters, head to the back (modern) staircase and climb to the top floor. As you descend, you'll pass by walls lined with fascinating original posters from those tough times.

Cost and Hours: Free, Mon-Fri 9:30-17:30, closed Sat-Sun, ask about guided tours, café, 17 Donegall Square North, +44 28 9032 1707, www.linenhall.com.

Donegall Square to the Cathedral Quarter

This little stroll through Belfast's shopping district takes you from City Hall to the Cathedral Quarter in 10 minutes or less.

Donegall Square: The front yard of City Hall is littered with statues of historic figures. Take a close look at the **Queen Victoria** monument (front and center). It celebrates the industrial might of Belfast: shipping, linen (the woman with the bobbin), and education (the student). Around the building to the right (as you face Queen Victoria) is a reminder of how Belfast was a springboard for the European battlefront in World War II—a **monument** dedicated by General Dwight D. Eisenhower in 1945 to the more than 100,000 US troops who were stationed in Northern Ireland. And around City Hall to the left (as you face the building), you'll find the thought-provoking **Titanic Memorial Garden.**

Donegall Place: City Hall faces the commercial heart of Belfast. With your back to City Hall, follow Queen Victoria's gaze across the square and down the shopping street called Donegall Place (note the **TI** on the left). Victoria would recognize the fine 19th-century brick buildings—built in the Scottish Baronial style when the Scots dominated Belfast. But she'd be amazed by the changes since then. As a key shipbuilding and industrial port, Belfast was bombed by the Germans in World War II. (On the worst night of bombing more than 900 died.) And, with the Troubles killing the economy in the last decades of the 20th century, little was built. With peace in 1998—and government investing to subsidize that peace—the 21st century has been one big building boom.

Walk down Donegal Place past the **eight stylized sails** celebrating the great ships built here for the White Star Line (their names all end in "ic").

Shopping Streets: At the sail for the *Celtic,* cruise to the right down Castle Lane. This is the busker zone, alive with street music on nice days. Ahead is the striking, modern **"Spirit of Belfast" statue** (a.k.a. the "Onion Rings"). That "spirit" is the spirit of industry—specifically linen and shipbuilding (light and strong, like the statue). The spirit could also be the resilience of this city with its complicated history.

To the right of the statue (down William Street) is the sleek and modern **Victoria Square Shopping Center,** worth a visit for

BELFAST

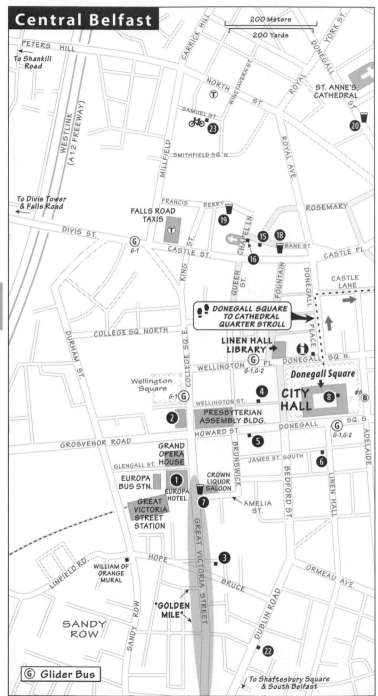

Central Belfast

200 Meters
200 Yards

PETERS HILL

To Shankill
Road

WESTLINK (A12 FREEWAY)

CARRICK HILL

NORTH ST.
WINETAVERN ST.

DONEGALL ST.

YORK ST.

ROYAL

ST. ANNE'S
CATHEDRAL

SAMUEL ST.
(T)

23

SMITHFIELD SQ. N.

MILLFIELD

ROYAL AVE.

ROSEMARY

20

To Divis Tower
& Falls Road

DIVIS ST.

FRANCIS

FALLS ROAD
TAXIS
(T)

BERRY

19

KING ST.

CHAPEL LN.

15 18

CASTLE PL.

CASTLE ST.

16

BANK ST.

(G)
G-1

DURHAM ST.

COLLEGE SQ. NORTH

QUEEN ST.

FOUNTAIN ST.

DONEGALL PLACE

CASTLE LANE

DONEGALL SQUARE
TO CATHEDRAL
QUARTER STROLL

COLLEGE SQ. E.

LINEN HALL
LIBRARY

Wellington
Square

WELLINGTON PL.
(G)
G-1,6-2

DONEGALL SQ. N.

(i)

Donegall Square

(G)
G-1

WELLINGTON ST.

4

CITY
HALL

8

#B

2

PRESBYTERIAN
ASSEMBLY BLDG.

HOWARD ST.

DONEGALL

SQ. S.

(G)
G-1,6-2

GROSVENOR ROAD

BRUNSWICK ST.

5

JAMES ST. SOUTH

BEDFORD ST.

6

LINEN HALL

ADELAIDE

GRAND
OPERA
HOUSE

GLENGALL ST.

EUROPA
BUS STN.

1

EUROPA
HOTEL

GREAT
VICTORIA
STREET
STATION

CROWN
LIQUOR
SALOON

7

AMELIA
ST.

LINEFIELD RD.

WILLIAM OF
ORANGE
MURAL

HOPE

SANDY
ROW

SANDY ROW

GREAT VICTORIA STREET

3

BRUCE

"GOLDEN
MILE"

DUBLIN ROAD

ORMEAU AVE.

22

(G)   Glider Bus

To Shaftesbury Square
& South Belfast

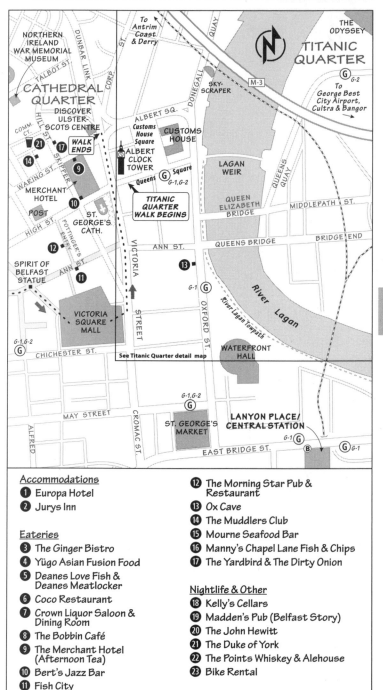

Accommodations
1 Europa Hotel
2 Jurys Inn

Eateries
3 The Ginger Bistro
4 Yūgo Asian Fusion Food
5 Deanes Love Fish & Deanes Meatlocker
6 Coco Restaurant
7 Crown Liquor Saloon & Dining Room
8 The Bobbin Café
9 The Merchant Hotel (Afternoon Tea)
10 Bert's Jazz Bar
11 Fish City

12 The Morning Star Pub & Restaurant
13 Ox Cave
14 The Muddlers Club
15 Mourne Seafood Bar
16 Manny's Chapel Lane Fish & Chips
17 The Yardbird & The Dirty Onion

Nightlife & Other
18 Kelly's Cellars
19 Madden's Pub (Belfast Story)
20 The John Hewitt
21 The Duke of York
22 The Points Whiskey & Alehouse
23 Bike Rental

its free elevator to the top of its glass dome offering grand city views (dome open Wed-Sun until 18:00). The center has lots of movies, restaurants, and shops (Mon-Sat 9:30-18:00, Thu-Fri until 21:00, Sun from 13:00).

Victoria Street: Exiting the mall, it's a short walk up Victoria Street to the Albert Memorial Clock Tower (and the start of my "Titanic Quarter Walk") and the Cathedral Quarter, described later in this section.

The Golden Mile

The Golden Mile is the overstated nickname of a Belfast entertainment zone with a few interesting sights on Great Victoria Street, just southwest of City Hall.

The **Presbyterian Assembly Building,** a fine example of Scottish Baronial architecture, has a welcoming little visitor exhibition that tells the story of the Presbyterians in Northern Ireland. They were discriminated against (like the Roman Catholics) because they also refused to embrace the High Church approach to Christianity as dictated by the Anglican Church (free, Mon-Fri 9:30-17:00, closed Sat-Sun, across from Jurys Inn at 2 Fisherwick Place).

The **Grand Opera House,** originally built in 1895, bombed and rebuilt in 1991, and bombed and rebuilt again in 1993, is extravagantly Victorian and *the* place to take in a concert, musical, play, or opera (ticket office open Mon-Sat 10:00-17:00, closed Sun; ticket office to right of main front door on Great Victoria Street, 44 28 9024 1919, www.goh.co.uk). Next door, the grand **Europa Hotel** is considered to be the most-bombed hotel in the world (33 times during the Troubles).

The **Crown Liquor Saloon** is the ultimate gin palace. Built in 1849 (when Catholic Ireland was suffering through the Great Potato Famine), its mahogany, glass, and marble interior is a trip back into the days of Queen Victoria. Wander through and imagine the snugs (booths designed to provide a little privacy for un-Victorian behavior) before the invasion of selfie-snapping tourists. Upstairs, the recommended Crown Dining Room serves pub grub and is decorated with historic photos.

Cathedral Quarter

Tucked between St. Anne's Cathedral and the River Lagan, this rejuvenating district is busy with shoppers by day and clubbers by night. And, being the oldest part of Belfast, it's full of history. Before World War I, this was the whiskey warehouse district—at a time when the Belfast region produced about half of all Irish whiskey.

While today's Cathedral District has a few minor sights, the big attraction is its nightlife—restaurants, clubs, and pubs. For the

epicenter of this zone, head for the intersection of **Hill Street and Commercial Court** and peek into nearby breezeways. As you explore, you'll find a maze of narrow streets, pubs named for the colorful characters that gave the city its many legends, and creative street-art murals that hint at the artistic spirit and still-feisty edginess of Belfast.

The Cathedral Quarter extends to the old merchant district, with its Victorian-era **Customs House** backed up to the river.

Nearby, at the intersection of High Street and Victoria Street, is Belfast's "Little Big Ben," the **Albert Memorial Clock Tower.** The tower was finished in 1869 to honor Queen Victoria's beloved Prince Albert, who died in 1861. It sits on the birthplace of the city, where Belfast was founded over a thousand years ago on a little river that later became High Street. (The little river still runs under the street.) The tower famously leans (as it was built on an unstable riverbank), and locals say Albert looks like he's ready to leap to safety when the tower finally falls.

About 50 yards in front of Albert is **St. George's Church** (with an interesting history posted at its gate). A church has stood here for over a millennium.

The clock tower is the start of my "Titanic Quarter Walk" (see page 82).

St. Anne's Cathedral

Also known as Belfast Cathedral, this Anglican church was built in the early 1900s, at the peak of Belfast's industrial power. Its mosaics and stained glass are colorful and modern. Lord Edward Carson, the fervent Unionist attorney who put Oscar Wilde behind bars—and whose Machiavellian political maneuverings ensured the creation of Northern Ireland in 1921—is buried here. The structure was nearly destroyed by a Luftwaffe bomb in 1941.

BELFAST

1916

This pivotal year means vastly different things to Northern Ireland's two communities. When you say "1776" to most Americans, it means revolution and independence from tyranny. But when you say "1916" to someone in Northern Ireland, the response depends on who's talking.

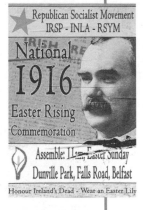

To Nationalists (who are usually Catholic), "1916" brings to mind the Easter Rising—which took place in Dublin in April of that year and was the beginning of the end of 750 years of British rule for most of Ireland. Some Nationalist murals still use images of Dublin's rebel headquarters or martyred leaders like Patrick Pearse and James Connolly. To this community, 1916 emphasizes their proud Gaelic identity, their willingness to fight to preserve it, and their stubborn anti-British attitude.

To Unionists (who are usually Protestant), "1916" means the brutal WWI Battle of the Somme in France, which began that July. (For more on the Somme, visit the Somme Museum in Bangor.) Although both Catholic and Protestant soldiers died in this long and costly battle, the first wave of young men who went over the top were the sons of

proud Ulster Unionists. The Unionists hoped this blood sacrifice would prove their loyalty to the Crown—and assure that the British would never let them be gobbled up by an Irish Nationalist state (a possible scenario just before the Great War's outbreak). You'll see Tommies heroically climbing out of their trenches in some of Belfast's Unionist murals. For the Unionists, 1916 is synonymous with devout, almost righteously divine, Britishness.

Today, the sleek "Spire of Hope" (added in 2007) is a 130-foot-tall witness to God's love of Belfast—in the form of a spike like the Spire in Dublin—but much shorter. Goofy nicknames are an Irish passion: This one's dubbed "The Rod to God."

Cost and Hours: £2 entry fee, £5 includes audioguide or personal guided tour (email ahead to book, admin@belfastcathedral.org); Mon-Sat 10:30-16:00, closed Sun except to worshippers; Sun

service at 11:00 and evensong at 15:30, Donegall Street, +44 28
9032 8332.

Northern Ireland War Memorial

Across the street from St. Anne's, this one-room sanctuary is dedicated to the lives lived and lost in this corner of the UK during
World War II. Coverage includes the American troops based here
during the war and the damage done by multiple German bombing
raids during the Blitz.

Cost and Hours: Free, Mon-Fri 10:00-16:00, Sat from
12:00, closed Sun, 21 Talbot Street, +44 28 9032 0392, www.
niwarmemorial.org.

Discover Ulster-Scots Centre

This bright and inviting gallery is designed to promote Ulster-Scots
heritage. Ulster and Scotland are 12 miles apart, and this exhibit
feels almost like propaganda, asserting that prehistoric Scots mi-
grated from northeastern Ireland—thus, the cultures are rightfully
intertwined. This center drills home the impact Ulstermen and
women had in building America, and if your heritage is Scots-Irish
(as they became known in America), it's a good place to begin your
genealogy research.

Cost and Hours: Free, Mon-Fri 10:00-16:00, closed Sat-Sun,
one block from clock tower at 1 Victoria Street, +44 28 9043 6710,
http://discoverulsterscots.com.

The Merchant Hotel

One of the finest buildings in town (16 Skipper Street), this was
once the headquarters of the Ulster Bank. Back when this was built

(mid-1800s), banks were designed with
over-the-top extravagance to give their
aristocratic clientele confidence. In
modern times, banking has changed,
and all over Britain such dazzling
mansions of finance have been vacated
and often turned into fancy restaurants. The hotel's recommended Bert's
Jazz Bar is famous for its cocktails,
and in the Great Room, under a grand
dome and the largest chandelier in Ireland, people dress up for the ritual of
afternoon tea (see "Eating in Belfast,"
later). You're welcome to poke around.

Understanding Belfast's Sectarian Neighborhoods

For centuries, Ireland has lived with tensions between Loyalists (also called Unionists, generally Protestants, who want to remain part of the United Kingdom, ruled from London) and Republicans (also called Nationalists, generally Roman Catholics, who want to be part of a united Ireland, independent from Great Britain). The Catholic Irish are the indigenous Irish and the Protestant loyalists are later arrivals, mostly "Scotch Irish," planted by London from Scotland in the north of Ireland.

A flare-up of violence in 1969 between these two communities led to a spontaneous mass reshuffling of working-class people in Belfast. Those who were minorities decided it was too dangerous to stay in the "wrong" sectarian neighborhood and moved into districts where they would be among their "tribe." Protestants left the Falls Road area for the Shankill Road area and Catholics left the Shankill Road area for the Falls Road area.

It's said that in these neighborhoods, the Catholics became more Irish than the Irish and the Protestants became more British than the British. Fighting between the two districts led the British army to build a "peace wall" to keep them apart. Paramilitary organizations on each side incited violence, and what came to be known as the Troubles began.

With two newly created ghettos dug in, it was a sad and bloody time that lasted until the Good Friday Agreement in 1998. Since then, the bombings, assassinations, and burnings have stopped, and peace has had the upper hand.

But Belfast is still segregated. Most working-class Protestants live and go to school with only Protestants. And the same is true in the Catholic community. The two groups have no trouble working or even socializing together downtown, but at night they retreat to their separate enclaves.

There is peace now. But there is no forgiveness: Murderers still cross paths with their victims' loved ones. Locals say it'll take another generation to be truly over the Troubles.

East of Donegall Square
▲St. George's Market

This was once the largest covered produce market in Ireland. Today the farmers are gone and everyone else, it seems, has moved in. Three days a week (Fri-Sun, about 9:00 until 14:00 or 15:00) St. George's Market becomes a thriving arts, crafts, and flea market. With a diverse array of street food, produce, and homemade goodies, it's a fun place for lunch (five blocks east of City Hall, at the corner of Oxford and East Bridge streets, +44 28 9043 5704).

SECTARIAN NEIGHBORHOODS IN WEST BELFAST

This slowly rejuvenating section of gritty West Belfast is home to two sectarian communities, living along the main roads to either side of a still-standing peace wall: Unionist/Loyalists/Protestants along Shankill Road and Republicans/Nationalists/Catholics along Falls Road.

There's plenty to see in the sectarian hoods—especially murals. While you could simply (and safely) walk through these districts on your own, I find it more meaningful to have a guide and hear firsthand, personal perspectives.

Here I list my recommendations for touring the sectarian neighborhoods, then describe the sights you'll see along the way. Before you go, read the "Understanding Belfast's Sectarian Neighborhoods" sidebar to give context to your visit.

Touring the Sectarian Neighborhoods

Touring the Republican and Loyalist areas is a ▲▲▲ experience, and there are several ways you can do it: via taxi tour, on foot with a guide, or on your own (using cabs as you go). Glider buses and hop-on, hop-off bus tours also drive these roads but are impersonal and don't let you meet locals.

Sectarian Neighborhood Taxi Tours

Taxi tours are easy and, for me, the most interesting way to spend a couple of hours in Belfast. Your driver/guide will take you around to various sights in both communities and give you running commentary (which, depending on your guide, can be heavily biased).

Falls Road Taxi Service: The **Belfast Taxis CIC** (formerly West Belfast Taxi Association, or WBTA), run by a group of local Falls Road (Republican) men, is located in the car park at the intersection of Castle and King streets (35a King Street). On the ground floor of this nine-story parking garage, a passenger terminal connects travelers with old black cabs—and the only Irish-language signs in downtown Belfast. From here, you can either take a shared black cab along Falls Road or hire a private driver.

By Shared Cab: Five-passenger black cabs shuttle residents from outlying neighborhoods up and down Falls Road and to the city center. All shared cabs go up Falls Road, past Sinn Féin headquarters and lots of murals, to the Milltown Cemetery (try sitting

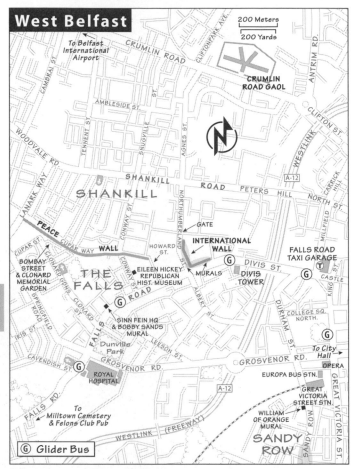

in front so you can chat with the cabbie). It's £1.50/ride (pay driver in cash). You can get a cab at the passenger terminal (cabs leave when they fill up), or anywhere along Falls Road (look for black cars with their roof signs removed). You may have to wait a bit for one to come by; when you see one, flag it down. When you want to get out, rap on the window.

This service originated more than 50 years ago at the beginning of the Troubles, when locals would hijack city buses and use them as barricades in the street fighting. Because of this, city bus service was discontinued, and local sectarian groups established a shared taxi service.

By Private Tour: If you want a tour guide, the same cab drivers described above can also be hired for 90-minute private tours, in which they show you around Republican-area sights and also take you into the Loyalist zone (remember that these drivers are Republican when listening to their viewpoints). To hire a driver for a private tour, just show up to the passenger terminal described above and ask the dispatcher (£45 for three people, £15/additional person, arrive by 18:00, can also be booked online for additional charge, pay drivers in cash, +44 28 9031 5777 or +44 78 9271 6660, www.taxitrax.com).

Cab Tours Belfast: This group of driver/guides from both communities (Catholic and Protestant) has teamed up and is committed to giving unbiased dual-narrative tours. Their "Belfast Murals Tour" covers both neighborhoods and is a fascinating 90 minutes (£45 for two people, tours run regularly daily 8:00-17:00, book online, free pickup/drop-off at Jurys Inn Great Victoria

Street or City Hall, extra charge for hotel pickup, +44 77 1364 0647, www.cabtoursbelfast.com).

Belfast Political Tours: This company, which also offers a guided walk (described below), runs taxi tours told from both sides. Riders switch taxis and guides at the halfway point to get two different perspectives (£100, 2.25 hours, 3-5/day, +44 73 9358 5531, www.belfastpoliticaltour.com).

Sectarian Neighborhood Walking Tours

On your own, get a map and lace together the stops described later (under "Sights in the Sectarian Neighborhoods"). Walking mixes well with hopping into shared taxis that go up and down Falls Road (described earlier). Or consider one of the following **walking-tour companies.**

Coiste Irish Political Tours offers the Republican community perspective on a three-hour "Falls Road Mural" walking tour. Led by Republicans who were once political prisoners, the tours visit murals, gardens of remembrance, and peace walls. Tours meet at the Coiste mural at Divis Tower on Divis Street and end at Milltown Cemetery. Afterwards, you're invited for a complimentary glass of Guinness at the Felons Club Pub—also run by Republican ex-prisoners (£12; Tue, Thu, and Sat-Sun at 10:00; best to book in advance, +44 28 9020 0770, www.coiste.ie).

Belfast Political Tours runs a walking tour called "Conflicting Stories" in which former combatants from each side show and tell their story: a Republican for Falls Road sights and then a Unionist for Shankill Road sights (£23, 3 hours, most days at

BELFAST

14:30, departs from Divis Tower; see contact info above http://www.belfastpoliticaltours.com/).

Sights in the Sectarian Neighborhoods

The sectarian neighborhoods are known for their murals. People here are working class and most live in row houses. The end of a row house is ready-made for a big political mural—and there are lots of them.

It's a land where one community's freedom fighter is another community's terrorist. Although fighters didn't actually wear military uniforms, they're often portrayed in uniform in proud murals. (Near Shankill Road there are still murals that celebrate "Top Gun" patriots who killed lots of Roman Catholics.)

But with more peaceful times, the character of these murals is slowly changing. The government is helping fund programs that replace aggressive murals with positive ones. Paramilitary themes are gradually being covered over with images of pride in each neighborhood's culture. The *Titanic* was built primarily by proud Protestant Ulster stock and is often seen in their neighborhood murals—reflecting their industrious work ethic. And in the Catholic neighborhoods, you'll see more murals depicting mythological heroes from the days before the English came.

Shankill Road Area

Walking down the main part of Shankill Road (around Agnes and Conway streets), you'll see murals, memorials to people killed, and lots of red, white, and blue. In this area you also may see fields where bonfires are built, with piles of wood awaiting the next Orange Day, July 12—when Protestants march and burn huge fires (and when Catholics choose to leave town on vacation). At the edge of the area is the Crumlin Road Gaol, a prison where combatants (mostly Republicans) did time (described next).

▲Crumlin Road Gaol

This Victorian-era jail was kept busy from 1846 to 1996 incarcerating people—men, women, and even children. Its purpose: to control the angry indigenous Irish. Exhibits and re-creations now provide an interesting look at how the prison was run, who was held here, and what life was like for the prisoners.

Cost and Hours: £12, daily 10:30-17:00, Fri-Sat until 18:30 in summer, last entry two hours before closing; they also offer a guided tour, plus a combo-tour of the sectarian neighborhood and jail (either by taxi or on foot)—see the website for more on these options; coffee stand, pub, +44 28 9074 1500, www.crumlinroadgaol.com.

Getting There: The jail is at 53 Crumlin Road, a half-mile north of Shankill Road. It's about a 25-minute walk from the city center. It's easiest to take a taxi (also doable by bus—use the journey planner on www.translink.co.uk).

Visiting the Jail: The jail visit follows a one-way route through the prison. You'll get a look at the tunnel that connected the jail to the (now derelict) courthouse across the street and enter the Circle (the central area from which the four cell wings spoke out). Along the way, you'll meet the prison warder and governor as holograms, who provide insight into prison life and operations.

From the Circle, you'll stroll down C Wing, which now holds re-creations of various cells (from 1846, the 1970/80s, and a child prisoner's cell), and also models of other spaces (officials' offices, kitchen, bathroom). Other cells host video exhibits covering topics such as prisoner accounts, executions, and hard labor in Victorian times. In the Troubles exhibit, a simple but effective animated video details the entire history of Northern Ireland's sectarian divide.

Finally, you'll head outside for a loop around the prison wall to see where executed prisoners were buried in unmarked graves. The visit ends with a look at a Westland Wessex helicopter and the role of the British army and RAF at the jail.

Peace Wall

A sad, corrugated peace wall runs a block or so north of Falls Road (along Cupar Way), separating the Catholics from the Protestants in the Shankill Road area.

The most prominent of Belfast's peace walls, this one has five gates that are shut in the evenings. On the Loyalist side of the wall is a long stretch featuring colorful art and messages of peace and hope, added by tourists.

The first wall here was cement and 20 feet high; it was later extended another 10 feet by a solid metal addition, and then another 15 feet with a metal screen. Seemingly high enough now to deter a projectile being lobbed over, this is one of many such walls erected in Belfast during the Troubles. Meant to be temporary, these barriers stay up because of old fears among the communities on both sides.

Falls Road and Nearby

In the Catholic Falls Road area, you'll notice that the road signs are in two languages (Irish first). Sights include the many political murals, neighborhood memorial gardens, and Bombay Street, which the Protestants burned in 1969, igniting the Troubles. Next to the well-fortified Sinn Féin Press Office is a political gift-and-

BELFAST

book shop. The powerful local Republican museum is two blocks away. Farther down Falls Road is the Milltown Cemetery, where the hunger strikers are buried and revered as martyrs (all described next).

International Wall: At the corner of Falls Road and Northumberland Street stretches the colorful, so-called International Wall, an L-shaped, two-block-long series of political murals that not only pays tribute to Republican heroes but also shows solidarity with other oppressed groups. Along the Falls Road section of the International Wall are murals dedicated to recent local events and causes. If you walk down Northumberland Street a few blocks from the wall, you'll reach a set of gates, with peace messages and art, that lead to the Loyalist side.

Sinn Féin Press Office: Near the bottom of Falls Road, at #51, is the press center for the hardline Republican party, Sinn Féin. While the press office is not open to the public, the adjacent **bookstore** (with an intriguing gift shop) is welcoming and worth a look. Page through books featuring color photos of the political murals that decorated these buildings. Money raised here supports the families of deceased IRA members.

Around the corner is a big and bright mural remembering **Bobby Sands,** a member of parliament who led a hunger strike in prison with fellow inmates and starved himself to death to very effectively raise awareness of the Republican concerns.

Eileen Hickey Republican History Museum: This volunteer-run museum, tucked away in a residential complex, has a clear mission: "For Republican history to be told by Republicans. To educate our youth so they may understand why Republicans fought, died, and spent many years in prison for their beliefs." This is an unforgettable museum, with real (if totally biased) history shown and told by people who played a part in it (free, Tue-Sat 10:00-14:00, closed Sun-Mon, two blocks from Sinn Féin Press Office at 5 Conway Place, +44 28 9024 0504, www.eileenhickeymuseum.com).

Bombay Street and Clonard Memorial Garden: About a 10-minute walk from the Sinn Féin Press Office is Bombay Street and the Clonard Memorial Garden. On August 15, 1969, Loyalists set fire to the Catholic homes and a monastery on this street. In the violence, a Republican teenager was killed. The burning of this Catholic street led to the "sorting out" of the communities and the building of a peace wall. Today you'll see Bombay Street nicely rebuilt, photos of the terrible event, and a peaceful memorial garden against the wall.

Milltown Cemetery: This burial site for Republican martyrs can be a pilgrimage for some. You'll walk past all the Gaelic crosses down to the far right-hand corner (closest to the highway), where little green railings set apart the IRA Roll of Honor from the thousands of other graves. These martyrs are treated like fallen soldiers. Notice the memorial to Bobby Sands and nine other hunger strikers. They starved themselves to death in the nearby Maze Prison in 1981, protesting for political prisoner status as opposed to terrorist criminal treatment; the prison closed in the fall of 2000. The cemetery is a long 35-minute walk from the Sinn Féin Press Office; you're better off taking a Falls Road taxi or the #G1 Glider to the Falls Park stop (cemetery open daily 9:00-16:00, 546 Falls Road, +44 28 9061 3972).

Sandy Row

To the southwest of City Hall, Sandy Row is a smaller Unionist, Protestant working-class street just behind the Europa Hotel that offers a cheap and easy way to get a dose of a sectarian neighborhood. From the Europa Hotel, walk a block down Glengall Street, then turn left and walk for 10 minutes. A stop in a Unionist memorabilia shop, a pub, or one of the many cheap eater-

ies here may give you an opportunity to talk to a local. Along the way you'll see murals filled with Unionist symbolism. The mural of William of Orange's victory over the Catholic King James II (Battle of the Boyne, 1690) thrills Unionist hearts (at the northern end of Sandy Row at the corner with Linfield Road).

TITANIC QUARTER

At their height, the Belfast shipyards employed more than 30,000 people. But after World War II, with the advent of air travel and the rise of cheaper labor at shipyards located in Asia, shipbuilding declined here and moved to other parts of the world. The last ocean liner was built here in 1961 and the very last ship of any kind built here sailed away in 2003. The shipyards continually downsized; some were abandoned while others morphed into repair yards for other maritime endeavors like oil-rig and oceanic wind-turbine repair.

By the mid-1990s, the proud former shipbuilding district

along the River Lagan was a barren industrial wasteland. But during the Celtic Tiger boom years, shrewd investors saw the real-estate potential and began building posh, high-rise condos.

The first landmark project to be completed was the Odyssey entertainment complex (in 2000). To draw more visitors and commemorate the proud shipbuilding industry of the Victorian and Edwardian ages, another flagship attraction was needed. The 100th anniversary of the *Titanic* disaster in 2012 provided the perfect opportunity, and the result was the Titanic Belfast Museum, a phenomenally popular exhibition about the ill-fated ship. Today, the entire eastern bank of the Lagan is a riverfront promenade nicknamed "the Maritime Mile"—a delightful walk (described later).

While you can just go the Titanic Belfast Museum, if you have time, see the museum as part of my walk. The Glider #G2 from City Hall makes stops all along the way, including at the Titanic Belfast Museum and the HMS *Caroline*.

▲▲Titanic Quarter Walk

This self-guided walk takes about an hour, not including its two major stops: the Titanic Belfast Museum and the HMS *Caroline* (both described later).

• *Belfast's leaning* ❶ **Albert Memorial Clock Tower** *marks the start of this walk (for more about the clock tower, see page 71). From there, head for the River Lagan, where you'll find the...*

❷ Lagan Weir

The first step in rejuvenating a derelict riverfront is to tame the river, get rid of the tides, and build modern embankments. The star of that major investment is the Lagan Weir, the people-friendly gateway to the Titanic Quarter. Built in 1994, the weir is made up of four large pier houses and five giant gates that divide freshwater from saltwater and control the river's flow—no more flooding. The giant salmon sculpture is covered in words and images related to Belfast's history.

Now walk across the weir on the curving pedestrian footbridge (added in 2015). Notice how much lower the water is on the saltwater side of the weir (depending on the tide). Looking downstream, on the right, a popular riverside walk goes scenically inland from here 14 miles along the old tow path.

• *At the end of the bridge, you'll see* a Game of Thrones *stained-glass window on the right (one of several you will see on this walk). Belfast has six, commemorating the TV series, filmed here, that gave tourism in Northern Ireland a nice bump. Now head left.*

❸ Maritime Mile Walk

This parklike promenade laces together several sights along the riverbank. It's lined with historic photo plaques that tell the story of this industrial river. The far side of the river was busy with trade (importing and exporting), and this side was all about shipbuilding. All along the way you'll get glimpses (to the right) of the city's iconic and giant yellow cranes. The big *H&W*

stands for Harland and Wolff, Belfast's once-mighty shipyard, but locals just call them Samson and Goliath. (In 2019, the last 130 employees of Harland and Wolf saw their once-proud company file for bankruptcy.)

• *Continue walking until you reach the Odyssey arena complex.*

❹ The Odyssey

This huge millennium-project complex offers restaurants, a bowling alley, a 12-screen cinema, and the **W5 science center** with interactive, educational exhibits for kids. Where else can you play a harp with laser-light strings? The "W5" stands for "who, what, when, where, and why" (£13.50 for adults, £10 for kids, generally daily 10:00-18:00 in summer, shorter hours and closed Mon-Wed off-season, 2 Queen's Quay, +44 28 9046 7790, www.w5online. co.uk).

There's also the 12,000-seat **SSE Odyssey Arena,** where the Belfast Giants professional hockey team skates. The arena is all about boosting nonsectarian sports (like hockey) rather than traditionally Loyalist (cricket, rugby, soccer) or Republican (hurling, Gaelic football) sports that amp up anger between the tribes here. Under one giant roof, the entire city gets together—Loyalists and Republicans alike—and roots for the same team (matches are generally late Sept-mid-April on weekends, check website for ticket info, +44 28 9073 9074, www.belfastgiants.com).

• *Turning inland, you come to the* ❺ **Belfast Harbor Marina** *with an arc of shops and condos. On the corner are three huge buoys (buoy is pronounced "boy" in Britain). "The Belfast Buoys" (fondly called Tom, Dick, and Harry here) are described on info boards.*

At the far end of the arc of shops, find the **Dock Café,** a welcoming, convivial, and homey spot. Volunteer-run by local churches, its mission is to celebrate tolerance and "love your neighbor"— even if they practice a different religion. The coffee and cakes are wonderful, and you famously pay whatever you like at the donation box (though these days you can also donate electronically). There's soup and bread at lunchtime (Mon-Sat 11:00-16:00, possibly later in summer, closed Sun). You're welcome to bring in a picnic from

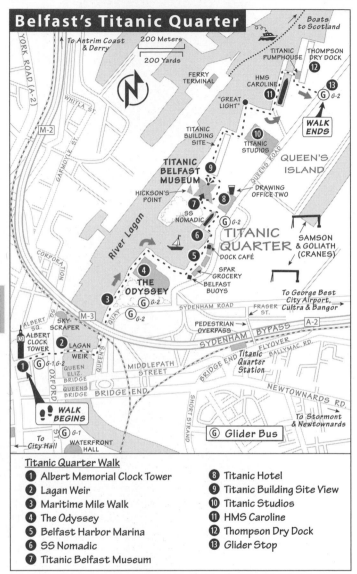

Belfast's Titanic Quarter

Titanic Quarter Walk

1. Albert Memorial Clock Tower
2. Lagan Weir
3. Maritime Mile Walk
4. The Odyssey
5. Belfast Harbor Marina
6. SS Nomadic
7. Titanic Belfast Museum
8. Titanic Hotel
9. Titanic Building Site View
10. Titanic Studios
11. HMS Caroline
12. Thompson Dry Dock
13. Glider Stop

the adjacent grocery store. Browsing the café's exhibits and displays and talking with its volunteers just makes you feel good here in a city with such a difficult story.

Another good (but for-profit) café called the Paper Cup lurks around the corner from the Dock.

• *Ahead looms the superstar of the Titanic Quarter, the Titanic Belfast Museum with its striking white-and-gray building—as tall as the mighty ship itself. As you approach, you'll pass a big ship that was just the tender (the shuttle dinghy) for the Titanic.*

❻ SS *Nomadic*

This ship once ferried passengers between the dock and the *Titanic*. Sitting in the dry dock where it was built, it's restored to appear as it was in 1912 when it shuttled Benjamin Guggenheim, John Jacob Astor, Molly Brown, and Kate Winslet to that fateful voyage (50 yards south of the Titanic Belfast Museum, entry included with your ticket).

• *Now is a good time to tour the* ❼ **Titanic Belfast Museum** *(see listing later). As you approach the museum, to the left of it is Hickson's Point, a small building that was originally a chapel, built to provide a space for reflection for visitors to the Titanic exhibit. That was expecting a bit much from the tourists—no one used it, and now it's a pub.*

After touring the museum, walk across the plaza (heading inland). Facing the museum is the entrance to the...

❽ Titanic Hotel

Housed in the former Harland and Wolff shipyard headquarters (known as the Drawing Office), this new hotel was permitted on condition that the public be allowed to wander through its historic spaces. For 150 years, many of the largest and finest ships in the world were designed here. Ask at the reception desk about the Art and Heritage Trail map, which provides a mini tour of the hotel. You'll see the private offices of some of the executives, an elegant presentation room, and the well-lit central Drawing Office Two, where the plans for the *Titanic* were drawn (now a pub and a fine place to have food or a drink). *Titanic* aficionados and maritime design geeks love this place.

• *Head toward the river. Stand at the back of the museum and look out at the place where the Titanic was actually built.*

❾ *Titanic* Building Site View

A big, stylized **map** in the pavement shows the route of the *Titanic*'s one and only voyage (just outside the museum's back exit). The brown benches are long and short—set up in dots and dashes to represent the Morse code distress transmissions sent on that fateful day. Just beyond two dashes, a few steps to the left, find (in the pavement) the symbolic steel tip of the ship; stand there looking out. This was where the bow was; the lampposts (stretching 300 yards before you) mark the size of the ship built here. Fifty yards ahead is a memorial with the names of all who perished.

• *Walk straight ahead toward the water, to what would have been the stern of the* Titanic.

❿ Titanic Studios

The giant warehouse-like building to your right was once the shipyard's Paint Hall, and is now Titanic Studios (not open to the public)—the soundstage where much of *Game of Thrones* was filmed. Continue past the *Game of Thrones* stained-glass window here (featuring the Iron Throne). following the waterfront path. Eventually you reach the Great Light, a lighthouse optic from a 1920s lighthouse (lit up at night). It was moved here from a

nearby island. (The info board enthralls lighthouse fans.)

• *Continue walking along the promenade. On the right, you'll reach the...*

⓫ HMS *Caroline*

A WWI battleship that fought in the 1916 Battle of Jutland, the HMS *Caroline* is one of only three surviving Royal Navy ships from that war, and well worth exploring (see listing, later). During World War II and later, the *Caroline* served as a headquarters and training ship until being decommissioned in 2011—the second-oldest ship in the Royal Navy's service.

• *Circle around the HMS* Caroline. *Past the ticket office, turn left, heading away from the river. On the left, you'll pass the...*

⓬ Thompson Dry Dock

This is the massive dry dock where the *Titanic* last rested on dry land. The Edwardian pump house filled the dry dock with water—and emptied it—in record time (26 million gallons in one hour). Slipways rolled new hulls down a slope into the water, where they were then towed to a dry dock. It's here that the final outfitting was completed, adding extra weight before the final watertight launch.

• *Walk out to the street and across it to find a* ⓭ **Glider stop.** *From here you can catch the #G2 back to City Hall, retracing much of what you just walked past with nice views of cranes and harbor action as you glide.*

Titanic Quarter Sights

▲▲▲Titanic Belfast Museum

This £97 million attraction stands right next to the original slipways where the *Titanic* was built. Creative displays tell the tale of the famous ocean liner, proudly heralded as the largest man-made moving object of its time. The sight has no actual artifacts from the underwater wreck (out of respect for the fact that it's a mass grave). The artifacts on display are from local shipbuilding offices and personal collections.

Cost and Hours: £21.50, includes entry to SS *Nomadic;* daily 9:00-18:00, June-Aug until 19:00, Oct-March 10:00-17:00, shorter hours for SS *Nomadic,* last entry 1 hour 40 minutes before closing; audioguide-£4, but you get plenty of info without it; +44 28 9076 6399, www.titanicbelfast.com.

Ticket and Crowd-Beating Tips: Entry to the museum is by time slot, so book ahead online to get the entry time you want and to avoid ticket lines. If you book ahead, you'll need to collect your tickets once you arrive (find a machine). If you haven't booked ahead, you should be able to walk right in—but at busy times, you might have to wait for an open slot later in the day. If lines are long and you haven't prebooked, try buying a ticket online while waiting. The museum is generally busiest 11:00-14:00, so visit outside those times if you can.

Getting There: From the Albert Memorial Clock Tower at the edge of the Cathedral Quarter, it's a 20-minute walk: Follow my "Titanic Quarter Walk" (described earlier). From Donegall Square, you can take the Glider bus (#G2, 2-4/hour). A taxi from the city center costs about £6.

Tours: The one-hour **Discovery Tour** explains the striking architecture of the Titanic Belfast Museum building and the adjacent slipways where the ship was built (£13, book ahead, runs 12:00 and 14:00 in peak season).

Eating: The ground floor includes a **$ Galley Express** (sandwich café) as well as **$$ The Pantry** (cafeteria-style, with salads and hot food). Choices nearby include the upscale **$$$ Drawing Office Two** pub, occupying the rooms where the ill-fated vessel was designed (across the lane in the Titanic Hotel), and the **Dock Café,** a church-run community center serving pay-what-you-like soup, bread, cake, and coffee (described in the walk).

Visiting the Museum: The spacey architecture of the Titanic Belfast Museum building is a landmark on the city's skyline. Six stories tall, it's clad in more than 3,000 sun-reflecting aluminum panels. Its four corners represent the bows of the many ships (most of which didn't sink) that were built in these yards during the industrial golden age of Belfast.

You'll follow a one-way route through the exhibit's nine galleries on six floors. Helpful "crew" (museum staff) are posted throughout to answer questions.

The museum starts by setting the stage, explaining the growth of Belfast through linen mills and other industries. Eventually it became a global powerhouse in shipbuilding thanks to Harland and Wolff, the company behind the *Titanic*.

Farther along, exhibits explain the complex process of constructing and launching a ship of this magnitude. On floor 4, the "shipyard ride" is a fun (if cheesy) five-minute gondola ride through a series of stories and videos that attempts to capture what it was like to be a worker building the ship. (There's usually a line, so if short on time, you may want to skip it, as there's still a lot to see.)

Continuing on, the shipyard exhibit features a model showing the layout of the massive shipyard; it's situated in a room with a big window overlooking the actual construction site (which you can visit after leaving the building). Next, you'll get a sense for what it would have been like to be a passenger on the *Titanic*, with displays about the opulence on board, re-creations of cabins, and a 3D fly-through tour of the ship from engine room and third class (bottom) to the dining room, then up into first class and the navigation bridge (top).

In the recounting of the disaster, you'll hear voices of survivors and read the Morse code transmissions sent after the ship hit the iceberg. The sinking is followed by a media frenzy and an investigation, which leads to reforms and regulations. Finally, in the 200-seat Discovery Theatre, the seven-minute *Titanic Beneath* video shows eerie footage of the actual wreckage sprouting countless "rusticles" 12,000 feet down on the ocean floor. Don't miss the see-through floor panels at the foot of the movie screen where the wreck passes slowly under your feet.

And what do the people of Belfast have to say about the ship they built that sank on her first voyage? "She was OK when she left."

SS *Nomadic*: After you're done, you are free to use your ticket to visit the SS *Nomadic*, moored across from the entrance to the museum. This tender boat to the *Titanic* gives you a small taste of what it was like on the mother ship, with some decor similarities and first- and second-class areas.

▲HMS *Caroline*

Launched in 1914, the HMS *Caroline* is the sole surviving ship of the greatest naval battle of World War I—the Battle of Jutland in the North Sea. Despite being the bloodiest day in British naval history, it's regarded as a victory over the German navy, which never challenged Britain again. Locals nicknamed the *Caroline* the "HMS *Never Budge*" because she's been moored here for decades—she finally was converted into a museum in 2016.

Cost and Hours: £13.50, includes audioguide, daily 10:00-17:00; for tickets, walk around the ship (inland) to the adjacent building—the old pump house for the Thompson Dry Dock; Alexandra Dock, Queen's Road, www.nmrn.org.uk.

Visiting the Ship: The one-way route starts with a fascinating exhibit, which includes a 10-minute *Jutland Experience* video. Then you'll enter the actual ship, restored as if time stopped in 1916 (dinner is still on the table). You're free to explore from the torpedo exhibit to the thunderous engine room.

SOUTH BELFAST
▲Ulster Museum

This is Belfast's most venerable museum. It offers an earnest and occasionally thought-provoking look at the region's history, with a cross-section of local artifacts.

Cost and Hours: £5 suggested donation; Tue-Sun 10:00-17:00, closed Mon; café, south of downtown, in the Botanic Gardens on Stranmillis Road, +44 28 9044 0000, www.nmni.com.

Visiting the Museum: Exhibits in this five-floor museum start on the top floor and spiral down through various topics. The top two floors are dedicated to art, the next floor down is dedicated to natural sciences, and the final two focus on history, with the Troubles covered at the end.

Art exhibits include beautifully crafted fine crystal, china, porcelain, and pottery, much of it made in Ireland. Several painting galleries focus on Irish artists, from the late 1800s to today.

In the nature collection, dinosaur skeletons lurk, stuffed wildlife play possum, and geology rocks. You'll see land and sea creatures big and small, old and new, and rare and common. Displays illustrate the geological formation of the island of Ireland, starting 600 million years ago, and trace how the Ice Age affected the local landscape.

Next the museum focuses on civilizations, with exhibits and artifacts spanning the centuries, from the Bronze Age to the Middle Ages. Don't miss the room dedicated to the mummy of a woman from Thebes, who lies in a glass case in the center. An interesting exhibit on the Spanish Armada tells the story of the *Girona*, which was shipwrecked off the Antrim Coast north of Belfast in 1588. Soggy bits of gold, silver, leather, and wood were salvaged from the *Girona* and are now on display.

From here, step down into the delicately worded history section. A highlight is the wall covered with antique text. On the left

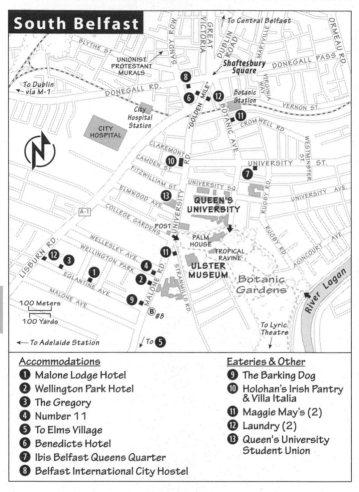

South Belfast

Accommodations
1. Malone Lodge Hotel
2. Wellington Park Hotel
3. The Gregory
4. Number 11
5. To Elms Village
6. Benedicts Hotel
7. Ibis Belfast Queens Quarter
8. Belfast International City Hostel

Eateries & Other
9. The Barking Dog
10. Holohan's Irish Pantry & Villa Italia
11. Maggie May's (2)
12. Laundry (2)
13. Queen's University Student Union

is the Ulster Covenant (1912), signed in blood by Unionist Protestants to resist incorporation into an independent Irish state. On the right is the Irish Proclamation of the Republic (1916), dear to Nationalist Catholic hearts as the moral compass of the Easter Uprising. Compare the passion of these opposing points of view.

Then continue through the coverage of the Troubles and beyond as this museum strives for balanced and thought-provoking reflections.

▲Botanic Gardens

This is the backyard of Queen's University, and on a sunny day, you couldn't imagine a more relaxing park setting. On a cold day, step into the Tropical Ravine for a jungle of heat and humidity. Take a quick walk through the Palm House, reminiscent of the one

The Red Hand of Ulster

All over Belfast, you'll notice a curious symbol: a red hand facing you as if swearing a pledge or telling you to halt. You'll spot

it, faded, above the Linen Hall Library door, in the wrought-iron fences of the Merchant Hotel, on old-fashioned clothes wringers (in the Ulster Folk Museum and Ulster Transport Museum at Cultra), above the front door of a bank in Bangor, in the shape of a flowerbed at Mount Stewart House, in Loyalist paramilitary murals, on shield emblems in the gates of Republican memorials, and even on the flag of Northern Ireland (the white flag with the red cross of St. George). It's known as the Red Hand of Ulster—and it is one of the few emblems used by both communities in Northern Ireland.

Nationalists display a red hand on a yellow shield as a symbol of the ancient province of Ulster. It was the official crest of the once-dominant O'Neill clan (who fought tooth and nail against English rule) and today signifies resistance to British rule in these communities.

But you'll more often see the red hand in Unionist areas. They see it as a potent symbol of the political entity of Northern Ireland. The Ulster Volunteer Force chose it for their symbol in 1913 and embedded it in the center of the Northern Irish flag upon partition of the island in 1921. You may see the red hand clenched as a fist in Loyalist murals. One Loyalist paramilitary group even named itself the Red Hand Commandos.

The origin of the red hand is a mythological tale of two rival clans that raced by boat to claim a far shore. The first clan leader to touch the shore would win it for his people. Everyone aboard both vessels strained mightily at their oars, near exhaustion as they approached the shore. Finally, in desperation, the chieftain leader of the slower boat whipped out his sword and lopped off his right hand...which he then flung onto the shore, thus winning the coveted land. Moral of the story? The fearless folk of Ulster will do *whatever it takes* to get the job done.

in London's Kew Gardens. The Ulster Museum is on the garden grounds.

Cost and Hours: Free, gardens open daily 8:00 until dusk, shorter hours for Palm House and Tropical Ravine, +44 28 9031 4762, www.belfastcity.gov.uk/parks.

Nearby: Just south of the gardens is the **Lyric Theatre,** an architecturally innovative building rebuilt in 2011 (no tours, but there are performances; see "Nightlife in Belfast," later).

BEYOND BELFAST
▲▲Ulster Folk Museum and Ulster Transport Museum

A sprawling 180-acre complex is home to two fine museums: the Ulster Folk Museum and the Ulster Transport Museum. The complex straddles the road and rail line at Cultra, midway between Bangor and Belfast (8 miles east of town).

Cost and Hours: Each museum is £9.90 for adults, £6.05 for kids ages 5 and up, family tickets available, online booking available but generally not necessary; Tue-Sun 10:00-17:00; Oct-Feb Tue-Fri 10:00-16:00, Sat-Sun from 11:00; closed Mon year-round; +44 28 9042 8428, www.nmni.com.

Getting There: From Belfast, it's a roughly £15 taxi journey or 15-minute drive (free and easy parking at both museums). By public transport, the bus is doable (use the journey planner at www.translink.co.uk), but the train is easy and reliable (2/hour, 15 minutes, from any Belfast train station or from Bangor, get off at Cultra). From the Cultra station it's just a few minutes' walk to the Transport Museum or a 15-minute walk uphill to the Folk Museum.

Planning Your Time: Plan to spend a couple of hours at each museum (a half-day total if seeing both). Consider the weather and plan accordingly. While the Transport Museum is mostly indoors, the Folk Museum is primarily outdoors and can involve lots of walking, with buildings spread across a hillside.

Ulster Folk Museum: Featuring 34 reconstructed buildings from all over the nine counties of Ulster, this open-air museum showcases the region's traditional lifestyles. First you can wander through the old town, dropping in at church, a print shop, schoolhouse, silent movie theater, bank, pub, and so on. There's also a tearoom in town that serves pastries and light lunches. From town, you can head into the country to nip into cottages, farmhouses, and mills. Some houses are warmed by a wonderful peat fire. Friendly attendants are stationed throughout. You might meet the blacksmith, carpenter, or basket weaver; talking to them can help bring the experience to life.

Ulster Transport Museum: This fine museum takes you through the history of various modes of transportation and features many models of old trains, trolleys, carts, cars, and more.

Most of the museum is contained in three seamlessly connected warehouse-like buildings. It starts with the **Rail Gallery,** where you'll enter onto a mezzanine above a world of model train cars. From there you'll descend a ramp to explore the history of trains and the Northern Ireland rail system, while wandering among various old train carriages.

The middle building holds the **Titanica** exhibit, which concisely covers the tale of the *Titanic,* from its inception in the shipyards of Belfast to its demise in the North Atlantic Ocean.

Next is the **Road Transport Gallery,** where you'll see an array of trolleys, trams, double-decker buses, and other types of street transport. From there, you'll descend farther into the car section, which covers more than a century of automobiles—everything from the Ford Model T to the bubble car (Beetles and Minis) to the "Cortina Culture" of the 1960s.

A separate building (down a long path) hosts the **Land, Sea, and Sky Galleries,** with an exhibit on carriages, caravans, and the two-wheeled cart. It also houses the **Museum of Innovation,** which celebrates local ties to great transportation breakthroughs. For instance, in 1909, the Belfast-based Shorts Aviation Company partnered with

the Wright brothers to manufacture the first commercially available aircraft. And in the early 1980s, the controversial automobile designer John DeLorean opened a factory in a suburb of Belfast to produce the DeLorean DMC-12. You can see a model of the DeLorean—presented as part of a high-tech sound and light show—at the museum.

▲Carrickfergus Castle

Built during the Norman invasion of the late 1100s, this historic castle stands sentry on the shore of Belfast Lough. William of

Orange landed here in 1690, when he began his Irish campaign against deposed King James II. In 1778, the American privateer ship *Ranger* (the first ever to fly the Stars and Stripes), under the command of John Paul Jones, defeated the HMS *Drake* just up the coast. These days the castle feels a bit sanitized and geared for kids, but it's an easy excursion if you're seeking a castle experience near the city.

Cost and Hours: £6, Tue-Sun 9:30-17:00, closed Mon, +44 28 9335 1273, https://discovernorthernireland.com (search for "Carrickfergus Castle").

Getting There: It's a 20-minute train ride from Belfast (on the line to Larne). Turn left as you exit the train station and walk straight downhill for five minutes—all the way to the waterfront—passing under the arch of the old town wall en route. You'll find the castle on your right.

▲The Gobbins Cliff Path

The Gobbins Cliff Path is an Edwardian-era adventure, replete with birds, beautiful scenery, and occasional rogue waves. Located 20 miles northeast of Belfast, beyond Carrickfergus, this complex path—a mix of tunnel bridges, railings, and steps carved, hammered, or fastened to the cliff—was first opened in 1902, designed to boost tourism. Once popular, it fell into disrepair during World War II and was closed for decades. The recently reinforced path (which, to spoil all the turn-of-the-century fun, now requires helmets and guides) takes two to three hours to hike, and is awkward and steep in places, but not terribly strenuous. You may spot puffins, cormorants, and kittiwakes in nesting areas along the way.

Cost and Hours: £20, visitors center open daily 8:30-17:00, required guided hikes generally run 1-2/hour from 9:30 or 10:00 until 14:30 (weather permitting), book in advance as tours can fill up, path closed Jan-Feb, +44 28 9337 2318, 68 Middle Road, Islandmagee, www.thegobbinscliffpath.com.

Getting There: By car, take A-2 from Belfast to Larne, turn right on B-90, and follow signs to *Islandmagee* and *The Gobbins*. Without a car, you can take a train from the Great Victoria Street station toward Larne. Get off at Ballycarry; the visitors center is a 20-minute signposted walk from there. By bus, from the Europa Bus Centre, you can ride bus #256 to Larne, transfer to bus #170b to Ballystrudder, and walk 15 minutes. Confirm schedules on Translink.co.uk; allow at least 1.5-2 hours if taking public transit.

Nightlife in Belfast

Theater

Located beside the River Lagan (near Queen's University), the **Lyric Theatre** is a Belfast institution. Rebuilt in 2011, it represents the cultural rejuvenation of the city—the building was partially funded by donations from actors such as Liam Neeson, Kenneth Branagh, and Meryl Streep. While there are no public tours, it's a good place to see quality local productions (tickets £15-30, box office open daily 10:00-17:00, 55 Ridgeway Street, +44 28 9038 1081, www.lyrictheatre.co.uk).

Traditional Music and Dance

Belfast Story features former *Riverdance* musicians and dancers in an energetic hour-long performance celebrating the people, poetry, and music of Belfast (call or go online for details, +44 79 7189 5746, www.belfasthiddentours.com, Conor Owens).

Musical Pub Crawl

The **Belfast Traditional Music Trail** is led by two local musicians. You'll walk to three fun venues in the Cathedral Quarter, where they play and explain traditional Irish music. It's a great intro to Irish music and Belfast's pulsing evening scene (£20, must book in advance, Sat at 16:00, 2.5 hours, meet at Second Fiddle, 42 Waring Street, +44 28 9028 8818, www.belfasttradtrail.com).

▲▲Live Music

A great way to connect with the people and culture of Belfast is over a beer in a pub. These places all add live music to the mix, making for an even cheerier atmosphere. Check pub websites to see what's on when you're in town.

Kelly's Cellars, once a rebel hangout (see plaque above door), still has a very gritty Irish feel. It's 300 years old and has a great fun-loving energy inside, a lively terrace, and Irish stew that's served until it runs out (daily until 24:00, live music nightly starting around 19:00 or 20:00, music also on Sat-Sun afternoons, tends to be trad during the week, anything goes on weekend evenings, 32 Bank Street, +44 28 9024 6058, https://kellyscellars.co.uk).

Madden's Pub is wonderfully characteristic, with a local crowd and trad music every night from 19:00 or 20:00 (no food, 2 blocks from Kelly's Cellars at 74 Berry Street, +44 28 9024 4114).

The John Hewitt is committed to the local arts scene—giving both musicians and artists a platform. They don't serve food but they do dish up live music almost nightly (51 Donegall Street, +44 28 9023 3768, www.thejohnhewitt.com).

The Duke of York is noisy for both eyes and ears—jammed with vintage mirrors and memorabilia, it feels like a drunken lamps-and-lighting store. To crank up the volume even more, they have live music nightly (from about 21:00 Mon-Thu, 17:00 Fri-Sun). It's on Commercial Court, the noisiest and most trendy/touristy street for nightlife in Belfast (7 Commercial Court, +44 28 9024 1062, www.dukeofyorkbelfast.com).

The Points Whiskey and Alehouse is an authentic Belfast pub, famed for its music—trad and Irish rock nightly after 22:00 (near the Europa Hotel at 44 Dublin Road, +44 28 9099 4124, www.thepointsbelfast.com).

Bert's Jazz Bar, at the Merchant Hotel, is good if you're in the mood for a cocktail in a plush, velvety Art Deco lounge with live jazz (from about 20:00 or 21:00, 16 Skipper Street, +44 28 9026 2713).

Sleeping in Belfast

Central Belfast is big, loud, and bustling. For quieter places and cozy guesthouses, check out the Queen's University area or the nearby seaside town of Bangor.

CENTRAL BELFAST

To locate these hotels, see the "Central Belfast" map on page 68.

$$$$ Europa Hotel is Belfast's landmark hotel—fancy, comfortable, and central—with four stars and 272 rooms. Modern yet elegant, this place is the choice of visiting diplomats (breakfast extra, Great Victoria Street, +44 28 9027 1066, www. hastingshotels.com, res@eur.hastingshotels.com).

$$$ Jurys Inn, an American-style hotel that rents 270 identical modern rooms, is perfectly located two blocks from City Hall (breakfast extra, Fisherwick Place, +44 28 9053 3500, www. jurysinns.com, jurysinnbelfast@jurysinns.com).

SOUTH BELFAST

To locate these hotels, see the "South Belfast" map on page 90.

South of Queen's University

Many of Belfast's quieter and less expensive accommodations are in a comfortable, leafy neighborhood just south of Queen's University (near the Ulster Museum). The Botanic, Adelaide, and City Hospital **train stations** are nearby (I find Botanic the most convenient), and buses zip down Malone Road every 10 minutes (less frequent on weekends). Any **bus** on Malone Road goes to Donegall Square East. **Taxis** take you downtown for about £8.

Located directly across University Road from the red-brick university building, One Elmwood is Queen's University's state-of-the-art **student union** (opened in 2022), with hangout spaces, a student store that sells food, a pub, and a rooftop garden. Grab a quick and cheap sandwich and coffee at **Clement's Coffee Shop** (closed Sun, 12 Elmwood).

$$$$ Malone Lodge Hotel, by far the classiest of the big-hotel listings in this neighborhood, provides slick, business-class comfort in 119 spacious rooms on a quiet street (breakfast extra, elevator, restaurant and bar, parking, 60 Eglantine Avenue, +44 28 9038 8000, www.malonelodgehotel.com, info@malonelodgehotel. com).

$$$ Wellington Park Hotel is a dependable, if unimaginative, chain-style hotel with 75 rooms in a good location (breakfast extra, pay parking, 21 Malone Road, +44 28 9038 1111, www. wellingtonparkhotel.com, info@wellingtonparkhotel.com).

$$ The Gregory, by the Warren Collection, ages gracefully in a stately red-brick Victorian house behind a green lawn. Located on a quiet street, with 16 large rooms decorated in soft colors, this place feels like an escape from the city (family rooms, parking, easy self check-in, 32 Eglantine Ave, +44 28 9099 5121, www. warrencollection.com, info@warrencollection.com).

$$ Number 11, by the Warren Collection, is in the same hotel family as the Gregory but has a more modern urban vibe. Housed in a four-story Victorian townhouse on the main road near the university, this place has 11 rooms with beautifully tiled bathrooms and techie accents, such as touch sensor mirrors (11 Malone Road, self check-in, same contact info as above).

¢ Elms Village, a huge Queen's University dorm complex, rents 100 basic, institutional rooms (all singles) to travelers during summer break (July and Aug only, coin-op laundry, self-serve kitchen; reception building is 50 yards down entry street, marked *Elms Village* on low brick wall, 78 Malone Road; +44 28 9097 4525, accommodation@qub.ac.uk; book via phone, email, or on www. hostelworld.com).

Between Queen's University and Shaftesbury Square

$$$ Benedicts Hotel has 32 rooms on three floors in a good location at the northern fringe of the Queen's University district. Its popular bar is a maze of polished wood and can be loud on weekend nights (includes breakfast if you book direct, elevator, 7 Bradbury Place, +44 28 9059 1999, www.benedictshotel.co.uk, info@ benedictshotel.co.uk).

$$ Ibis Belfast Queens Quarter, part of a hotel chain, has 56 practical rooms in a convenient location. It's a great deal if you're not looking for cozy character (breakfast extra, elevator, a block north of Queen's University at 75 University Street, +44 28 9033 3366, https://all.accor.com, h7288@accor.com).

¢ Belfast International City Hostel, big and creatively run, provides the best value among Belfast's hostels. It's near Botanic Station, in the heart of the lively university district, and has 24-hour reception. Paul, the manager, is a veritable TI, with a passion for his work (private rooms available, £5 cash key deposit taken, pay breakfast available at café, 22 Donegall Road, +44 28 9031 5435, www.hini.org.uk, info@hini.org.uk).

Eating in Belfast

CENTRAL BELFAST

For locations, see the "Central Belfast" map on page 68.

Fine Dining Near City Hall

$$$$ The Ginger Bistro serves a smart local crowd Irish/Asian cuisine with special attention to vegetarian and fish dishes. The casual front is for walk-ins, and the quieter, more romantic back is for those with reservations (Wed-Thu 17:00-21:00, Fri-Sat 12:00-21:30, closed Sun-Tue, 68 Great Victoria Street, +44 28 9024 4421, www.gingerbistro.com).

$$$ Yügo Asian Fusion Food is a foodie fave, trendy but with no pretense and lots of booze. The small dining room is tight with a dozen tables; eating at the bar gets you a fun view of the open kitchen. Their small plates (under £10) are good for sharing (vegetarian-friendly, Mon and Thu-Sat 12:00-15:00 & 17:00-21:30, closed Tue-Wed and Sun, reservations smart, 3 Wellington Street, +44 28 9694 7265, www.yugobelfast.com).

$$$$ Deanes Love Fish and **Deanes Meatlocker** are side-by-side sister eateries run by the powerhouse restaurateur Michael Deane, whose Michelin-star restaurant is next door. Each has a confident, impersonal vibe with good food in a classy atmosphere. I prefer Deanes Love Fish, with its minimalist, nautical feel. The Meatlocker is more for red meat and romance (Tue-Sat 12:00-15:00 & 17:00-21:30, closed Sun-Mon, one block from City Hall at 28 Howard Street, +44 28 9033 1134, www.michaeldeane.co.uk).

Other Options Near City Hall

$$$$ Coco Restaurant is a spacious place with a quirky sense of style, serving reliably tasty modern Irish and Continental dishes (open for dinner Wed-Sat from 17:30, lunch Wed-Fri 12:00-15:00, three-course fixed-price menu on Sun 13:00-19:00, good pre-theater menu until 18:30 Wed-Fri, closed Mon-Tue, a couple of blocks behind City Hall at 7 Linen Hall Street, +44 28 9031 1150, Tim).

$$ Crown Liquor Saloon and Dining Room is a dazzling gin palace on every sightseer's list. The ground-floor pub is a mesmerizing mishmash of mosaics and shareable snugs (booths—best to reserve), topped with a smoky tin ceiling. The dining room upstairs is similarly elegant but much quieter. Both serve the same pub grub, but upstairs seating comes with table service (downstairs 11:30-20:00,

upstairs 12:30-22:00, across from the Europa Hotel at 46 Great Victoria Street, +44 28 9024 3187, www.nicholsonspubs.co.uk).

Cheap Lunch at City Hall: $ The **Bobbin Café** is a good and cheery little cafeteria serving soups, sandwiches, and hot dishes (Mon-Fri 8:00-16:30, closed Sat-Sun, +44 28 9050 2068). A non-profit, they employ people with learning disabilities.

Cathedral Quarter and Nearby

In addition to the eateries listed here, there's a branch of Maggie May's that's open during the day (44 Castle Street; described later, under "Near Queen's University").

$$$$ The Great Room at the Merchant Hotel presents its afternoon tea in an expensive ritual. You'll enjoy velvety Victorian splendor under an opulent dome with a piano accompaniment. Sit under the biggest chandelier in Northern Ireland as you dine in the great hall of a former bank headquarters. If you've got a little money to burn, consider dressing up and indulging (£39.50/person, Mon-Fri 12:00-16:00, Sat seatings at 12:30 and 15:00, Sun 12:30-16:00, reservations smart, 16 Skipper Street, +44 28 9026 7963, www.themerchanthotel. com). They also do a dinner service of modern Irish/French cuisine.

$$$ Bert's Jazz Bar, also at the Merchant Hotel, is a fine option if you're looking for French cuisine served with jazz (daily generally 17:00-22:00, 16 Skipper Street, +44 28 9026 2713).

$$$ Fish City is a fine spot for its sustainably sourced, quality seafood dishes and attentive service. It has three dining spaces (one downstairs and two up), each with a different nautical vibe. The outdoor terrace, which spills onto a pedestrian street, is a delight on nice days. They host live music on weekend evenings in summer (daily 12:00-21:00, 33 Ann Street, +44 28 9023 1000, Grace).

$$ The Morning Star is a well-worn, once-elegant eatery with a characteristic pub on the ground floor (serving a hearty £6 lunch carvery Mon-Sat) and a low-energy dining hall upstairs. It has a good reputation for solid food in a historic pub (same pub-grub menu throughout, daily 12:00-22:00; down an alley just off High Street at 17 Pottinger's Entry, alley entry is roughly opposite the post office, +44 28 9023 5986).

$$ Ox Cave is a sleek and mod place with aproned French elegance. It was designed by the owners of the adjacent Michelin-starred Ox restaurant to entertain diners with wine and cheese as they wait for their table. But with charming Alain as your host, you could settle in here to make a meal from their charcuterie, cheese, small plates, and exciting wines. Order a glass, carafe, or bottle; this is your chance to try a less well-known wine (Wed-Sat 17:30-22:00, closed Sun-Tue, 3 Oxford Street, +44 28 9023 2567).

$$$$ The Muddlers Club, a loud, trendy, spacious, industrial-mod place, has an open kitchen and a fun format: a single, six-course set menu of international-style dishes that changes daily. Their wine-pairing option makes the tasting menu even better. Eating here is expensive, but it's a memorable slice of Belfast (Wed-Sat 17:00-21:30, also Fri-Sat lunch seatings at 12:30 & 13:00, closed Sun-Tue, reservations highly recommended, 1 Warehouse Lane, off Waring Street, +44 28 9031 3199, https://themuddlersclubbelfast.com).

$$$ Mourne Seafood Bar is my choice for seafood in an elegant setting with a fun staff and smart clientele. It's run by a marine biologist and a great chef—no gimmicks, just top-quality seafood (Wed 17:00-21:30, Thu-Sat 12:00-22:00, Sun 13:00-21:00, reservations smart, 34 Bank Street, +44 28 9024 8544, www.mourneseafood.com). As it's next to Kelly's Cellars (described earlier, under "Nightlife in Belfast"), consider dining here and then enjoying the music next door.

$ Manny's Chapel Lane Fish & Chips is a classic, cheap, neighborhood chippie (serving other fried food as well), with a small eat-in space in front (Mon-Sat 10:00-18:00, closed Sun, 11 Chapel Lane, +44 28 9031 9165).

$$ The Yardbird, rough and spacious, is housed in an open-beam attic. Their specialty is chicken (rotisserie and other), but they also have ribs and vegetarian options (daily 12:00-22:00, 3 Hill Street, +44 28 9024 3712). The **Dirty Onion** (downstairs) is a popular pub that spills suds and live music into its packed outer courtyard (you can bring in takeaway from the Yardbird). The Second Fiddle bar is off the courtyard.

NEAR QUEEN'S UNIVERSITY

For locations, see the "South Belfast" map on page 90.

$$$ The Barking Dog, elegant and inviting, serves small plates to be enjoyed family-style, along with pastas and local meat and seafood dishes. It's closest to my cluster of accommodations south of the university (Wed-Sat 12:00-14:30 & 17:00-22:00, Sun 12:00-20:00, closed Mon-Tue, near corner of Eglantine Avenue at 33 Malone Road, +44 28 9066 1885).

$$$ Holohan's Irish Pantry is like eating in a wealthy grandma's dining room. It's small with an inviting and nostalgic menu of Irish dishes—both classic (including boxty) and modern. The chef has a passion for seasonal ingredients (Tue-Sat 12:00-14:30 &

17:00-21:30, Sun 13:00-19:30, closed Mon, reservations smart, 43 University Road, +44 28 9029 1103, www.holohanspantry.co.uk).

$$ Villa Italia packs in crowds hungry for linguini and *bistecca*. Huge and family-friendly, with checkered tablecloths and a wood-beamed ceiling draped with grape leaves, it's a little bit of Italy in Belfast (Mon-Sat 17:00-22:00, Sun 12:30-20:30, reservations smart, three long blocks south of Shaftesbury Square, at intersection with University Street, 39 University Road, +44 28 9032 8356, www.villaitaliarestaurant.co.uk).

$ Maggie May's serves hearty, simple, affordable meals in a tight and cheery little bistro room. There are two locations near Queen's University, including one block south of Botanic Station (50 Botanic Avenue, +44 28 9032 2662) and near the Botanic Gardens (2 Malone Road, +44 28 9066 8515; both open Mon-Fri 8:00-20:30, Sat-Sun from 9:00).

Belfast Connections

BY TRAIN OR BUS

For schedules and prices for trains and buses in Northern Ireland, check with Translink (+44 28 9066 6630, www.translink.co.uk). Note that service is less frequent on Sundays.

From Belfast by Train to: Dublin (8/day, 2 hours), **Derry** (10/day, 2.5 hours), **Larne** (hourly, 1 hour), **Portrush** (hourly, 1.5 hours, transfer in Coleraine), **Bangor** (2/hour, 30 minutes).

By Bus to: Portrush (12/day, 2 hours; scenic-coast route, 2.5 hours), **Derry** (hourly, 2 hours), **Dublin** (hourly, most via Dublin Airport, 3 hours), **Galway** (every 2 hours, 5 hours, change in Dublin), **Glasgow** (3/day, 6 hours), **Edinburgh** (1/day, some direct, most with change, 7-8 hours). The Europa Bus Centre is on Glengall Street, behind the Europa Hotel.

BY PLANE

Belfast has two airports. **George Best Belfast City Airport** (code: BHD, www.belfastcityairport.com) is a 10-minute, £10 taxi ride from town (near the docks) or a £2.60 ride on the Airport Express bus #600 (2/hour from Europa Bus Centre). Meanwhile, **Belfast International Airport** (code: BFS, www.belfastairport.com) is 18 miles west of town—an £8 ride on the Airport Express bus #300 (3/hour from Europa Bus Centre).

If you're headed for Edinburgh or Glasgow, flying is generally better than taking the ferry (slow and not that scenic), as it's a fairly cheap, short trip.

It's also fast, cheap, and easy to get to Belfast directly from **Dublin Airport.** The **Aircoach** express bus runs in each direction, stopping at both Dublin Airport terminals and in downtown Belfast at the Europa Bus Centre on Glengall Street (next to the Europa Hotel and Great Victoria Street station). With this service you could spend your last night in Belfast and fly out of Dublin the next day (£14-16 from Belfast, runs every 1-2 hours, 2-hour ride, +44 28 9033 0655, www.aircoach.ie).

BY FERRY

Stena Line ferries connect Ireland with Scotland and England (+44 28 9074 7747, www.stenaline.co.uk). The **P&O Ferry** makes the run to Scotland (+44 1 304 448 888, www.poferries.com).

To Scotland: You can sail between Belfast and Cairnryan, Scotland, on the Stena Line ferry. A Rail Link coach connects the Cairnryan port to Ayr, where you'll catch a train to Glasgow Central station (6/day, 2.5 hours by ferry plus 2.5 hours by bus and train). The **P&O Ferry** goes from Larne, 20 miles north of Belfast, to Cairnryan (5/day, 2 hours), with bus or rail connections from there to Glasgow and Edinburgh. There are hourly trains between Belfast and Larne (1-hour trip).

To England: Stena Line ferries sail from Belfast to **Liverpool** (generally 2/day, 8 hours, arrives in port of Birkenhead—10 minutes from Liverpool).

Bangor

To stay in a laid-back seaside hometown—with more comfort per pound—sleep 12 miles east of Belfast in Bangor. With elegant old homes facing its spruced-up harbor and not even a hint of big-city Belfast, this town has appeal, and it's a handy alternative for travelers who find Belfast booked up by occasional conventions and conferences.

Formerly a Victorian resort and seaside escape from the big city nearby, Bangor now has a sleepy residential feeling. To visit two worthwhile sights near Bangor—the Somme Museum and Mount Stewart House—consider renting a car for the day at nearby George Best Belfast City Airport, a 15-minute train trip from Bangor.

GETTING THERE

Catch the train to Bangor from either Lanyon Place/Central or Great Victoria Street stations (2/hour, 30 minutes, go to the end of the line—don't get off at Bangor West). Consider stopping en route at Cultra (Ulster Folk Museum and Transport Museum; see

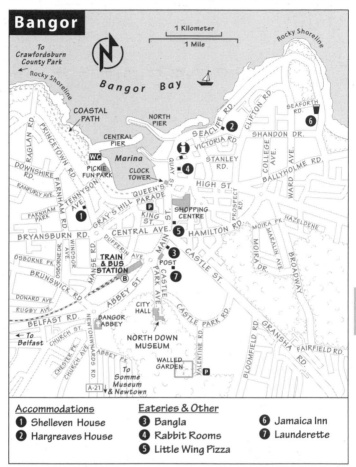

Bangor

To
Crawfordsburn
County Park

Rocky Shoreline

1 Kilometer

1 Mile

Bangor Bay

Rocky Shoreline

COASTAL
PATH

NORTH
PIER

CENTRAL
PIER

SEACLIFF RD.

CLIFTON RD.

SEAFORTH RD.

SHANDON DR.

VICTORIA RD.

STANLEY
RD.

COLLEGE AVE.

WARD AVE.

BALLYHOLME RD.

RAGLAN RD.

PRINCETOWN RD.

DOWNSHIRE
RD.

FARNHAM RD.

RANFURLY AVE.

TENNYSON AVE.

Marina

WC

PICKIE
FUN PARK

CLOCK
TOWER

QUEEN'S
PARADE

GRAY'S HILL

HIGH ST.

PROSPECT RD.

HAZELDENE

MOIRA PK.

FARNHAM
PARK

BRYANSBURN RD.

KING
ST.

CENTRAL AVE.

SHOPPING
CENTRE

HAMILTON RD.

MOIRA DR.

MARADIN AVE.

BROADWAY

OSBORNE PK.

WINDSOR DR.

MANSE RD.

DUFFERIN AVE.

MAIN ST.

CASTLE ST.

GRANSHA RD.

BRUNSWICK RD.

TRAIN
& BUS
STATION

ABBEY ST.

POST

CASTLE PARK AVE.

CASTLE PARK RD.

DONARD AVE.

RUGBY AVE.

CITY
HALL

BLOOMFIELD RD.

FAIRFIELD RD.

BELFAST RD.

CHESTER PK.

CHURCH ST.

NEWTOWNARDS RD.

BANGOR
ABBEY

NORTH DOWN
MUSEUM

VALENTINE RD.

To
Belfast

ABBEY PK.

CHURCH AVE.

To
Somme
Museum
& Newtown

A-21

WALLED
GARDEN

Accommodations
1 Shelleven House
2 Hargreaves House

Eateries & Other
3 Bangla
4 Rabbit Rooms
5 Little Wing Pizza

6 Jamaica Inn
7 Launderette

BELFAST

page 92). The journey gives you a good close-up look at the giant Belfast harbor cranes.

Orientation to Bangor

Tourist Information: Bangor's TI is in a stone tower house (from 1637) on the harborfront, a 10-minute walk from the train station (Mon-Fri 9:15-17:00, Sat from 10:00, closed Sun, 34 Quay Street, +44 28 9127 0069, www.discovernorthernireland.com, search for "Bangor Visitor Information Centre").

Helpful Hints: You'll find **Laundry Chute** at 2 Market Square, a block east of the train station, hidden next to a parking lot behind the post office—easiest access is from Main Street and up Market Street (Mon-Fri 9:00-17:30, Sat until 15:30, closed

Sun, +44 28 9146 5900). **Kare Cabs** provides local taxi service (+44 28 9145 6777). So does **Bangor Cabs** (+44 28 9145 6456).

Sights in Bangor

Walks

For sightseeing, your time is better spent in Belfast. But if you have time to burn in Bangor, enjoy a walk beside the water on the **Coastal Path,** which leads west out of town from the marina. A pleasant three-mile level walk along the water leads you to Crawfordsburn Country Park in the suburb of Helen's Bay. Hidden in the trees above Helen's Bay beach is Grey Point Fort, with its two WWI artillery bunkers guarding the shore. Allow 1.5 hours each way as you share the easy-to-follow and mostly paved trail with local joggers, dog walkers, and bikers.

For a shorter walk with views of the marina, head to the end of the **North Pier,** where you'll find a mosaic honoring a portion of the D-Day fleet that rendezvoused offshore in 1944, far from Nazi reconnaissance aircraft. Keep an eye out in the marina for Rose the seal. Little kids may enjoy the **Pickie Fun Park** next to the marina, with paddleboat swan rides and miniature golf. The **Bangor Castle** grounds are good for picnics and include a peaceful walled garden (free; grounds always open, garden Mon-Thu 10:00-20:00, Fri-Sun until 18:00, shorter hours off-season).

North Down Museum

This small museum covers local history, from monastic days to Viking raids to Victorian splendor. It's hidden on the grassy grounds behind City Hall, uphill and opposite from the train station.

Cost and Hours: Free, July-Aug daily 10:00-16:30; Sept-June Tue-Sat 10:00-16:00, Sun from 12:00, closed Mon; +44 28 9127 1200, www.northdownmuseum.com.

NEAR BANGOR

The eastern fringe of Northern Ireland is populated mostly by people who consider themselves true-blue British citizens with a history of loyalty to the Crown that goes back more than 400 years. Two sights within reach by car from Bangor highlight this area's firm roots in British culture: the Somme Museum and Mount Stewart House. Call ahead to confirm sight opening hours.

Getting There: Bus service from Bangor is patchy (15 minutes to Somme Museum, one hour to Mount Stewart House with transfer, best to check schedule with Bangor TI or www.translink. co.uk). I'd rent a car instead at nearby George Best Belfast City Airport, which is only 15 minutes by train from Bangor or 10 minutes from Belfast's Lanyon Place/Central Station. Because the airport is east of Belfast, your drive to these rural sights skips the headache of urban Belfast.

▲Mount Stewart House

No manor house in Ireland better illuminates the affluent lifestyle of the Protestant ascendancy than this lush estate. After the de-

feat of James II (the last Catholic king of England) at the Battle of the Boyne in 1690, the Protestant monarchy was in control—and the privileged status of landowners of the same faith was assured. In the 1700s, Ireland's many Catholic rebellions seemed finally to be squashed, so Anglican landlords felt safe flaunting their wealth in manor houses surrounded by utterly perfect gardens. The Mount Stewart House in particular was designed to dazzle.

Cost and Hours: £11 for house and gardens; house open daily 11:00-17:00, gardens from 10:00, closed Nov-Feb; 8 miles south of Bangor, just off A-20 beside Strangford Lough, +44 28 4278 8387, www.nationaltrust.org.uk/mount-stewart.

Visiting the House: In the **manor house,** you'll glimpse the cushy life led by the Marquess of Londonderry and his heirs over the past three centuries. The main entry hall is a stunner, with a black-and-white checkerboard tile floor, marble columns, classical statues, and pink walls supporting a balcony with a domed ceiling and a fine chandelier. In the dining room, you'll see the original seats occupied by the rears of European heads of state, brought back from the Congress of Vienna after Napoleon's 1815 defeat. A huge painting of Hambletonian, a prize-winning racehorse, hangs above the grand staircase, dwarfing a portrait of the Duke of Wellington

in a hall nearby. The heroic duke (worried that his Irish birth would be seen as lower class by British blue bloods) once quipped in Parliament, "Just because one is born in a stable does not make him a horse." Irish emancipator Daniel O'Connell retorted, "Yes, but it could make you an ass."

Afterward, wander the expansive manicured **gardens.** The fantasy life of parasol-toting, upper-crust Victorian society seems to ooze from every viewpoint. Fanciful sculptures of extinct dodo birds and monkeys holding vases on their heads set off predictably classic Italian and Spanish sections. An Irish harp has been trimmed out of a hedge a few feet from a flowerbed shaped like the Red Hand of Ulster. Swans glide serenely among the lily pads on a small lake.

Somme Museum

World War I's trench warfare was a meat grinder. More British soldiers died in the last year of that war than in all of World War II. Northern Ireland's men were not spared—especially during the bloody Battle of the Somme in France, starting in July 1916 (see the "1916" sidebar on page 72). Among the Allied forces was the British Army's 36th Ulster Division, which drew heavily from this loyal heartland of Northern Ireland. The 36th Ulster Division suffered brutal losses at the Battle of the Somme—of the 760 men recruited from the Shankill Road area in Belfast, only 10 percent survived.

Exhibits portray the battle experience through a mix of military artifacts, photos, historical newsreels, and life-size figures posed in trench warfare re-creations. To access the majority of the exhibits, it's essential to take the one-hour guided tour (leaving hourly, on the hour). Visiting this place is a moving experience, but it can only hint at the horrific conditions endured by these soldiers.

Cost and Hours: £7; July-Aug Mon-Fri 10:00-17:00, Sat from 11:00, last tour one hour before closing, closed Fri Sept-June and Sun year-round; 3 miles south of Bangor just off A-21 at 233 Bangor Road, +44 28 9182 3202, www.irishsoldier.org. A coffee shop is located at the center.

Sleeping in Bangor

Visitors arriving in Bangor (by train) come down Main Street, a 10-minute (mostly downhill) walk to reach the harbor marina. You'll find Hargreaves House up the east side of the harbor to the right, along the waterfront on Seacliff Road. The other two listings are to the left, closer to the train station and farther from the water. Take the first immediate left out of the station onto steeply downhill Dufferin Avenue; both are near the roundabout at the bottom.

$$$ Shelleven House is an old-fashioned, well-kept, stately place with 13 prim rooms on a quiet corner (RS%, family rooms, parking, 61 Princetown Road, +44 28 9127 1777, www. shellevenhouse.com, info@shellevenhouse.com, Sue and Paul Toner).

$$ Hargreaves House, a homey Victorian waterfront refuge with three cozy, refurbished rooms, is Bangor's best value, run by ever-helpful Pauline (RS%—use code "HHRS18," ocean views, parking, 15-minute walk from train station but worth it, 78 Sea-cliff Road, +44 28 9146 4071, mobile +44 79 8058 5047, www.hargreaveshouse.com, info@hargreaveshouse.com).

Eating in Bangor

Most restaurants in town stop seating at about 20:30.

$$$ Bangla serves fine Indian cuisine with attentive service and a good-value early-bird option before 19:00 (daily 12:00-14:00 & 16:30-23:00, 115 Main Street, +44 28 9127 1272).

$$ The **Rabbit Rooms** serves hearty Irish food to local crowds with live music after the dinner service several nights a week (daily 11:30-late, music Mon and Thu-Sat, near the harbor at 33 Quay Street, +44 28 9146 7699).

$ Little Wing Pizza is a friendly joint serving tasty pizza, pasta, and salads. Grab your food to go and munch by the marina. It's also one of the few places in town that serve food later at night (daily 11:00-22:00, 37 Main Street, +44 28 9147 2777).

The **$$ Jamaica Inn** offers pleasant pub grub and a breezy waterfront porch (food served about 12:00-21:00, 10-minute walk east of the TI, 188 Seacliff Road, +44 28 9147 1610).

BELFAST

PRACTICALITIES

This section covers just the basics on traveling in Northern Ireland (for much more information, see *Rick Steves Ireland*). You'll find free advice on specific topics at RickSteves.com/tips.

While it shares an island with the Republic of Ireland, Northern Ireland is part of the United Kingdom—which makes its currency, phone codes, and other practicalities different from the Republic.

MONEY

For currency, Northern Ireland uses the pound (£): 1 pound (£1) = about $1.30. One pound is broken into 100 pence (p). To convert prices in pounds to dollars, add 30 percent: £20 = about $26, £50 = about $65. (Check www.oanda.com for the latest exchange rates.) While the pound used here is called the "Ulster Pound," it's interchangeable with the British pound.

You'll use your **credit card** for purchases both big (hotels, advance tickets) and small (little shops, food stands). Visa and Mastercard are universal while American Express and Discover are less common. Some European businesses have gone cashless, making a card your only payment option.

A **"tap-to-pay"** or "contactless" card is the most widely accepted and simplest to use: Before departing, check if you have—or can get—a tap-to-pay credit card (look on the card for the symbol—four curvy lines) and consider setting up your smartphone for contactless payment. Let your bank know that you'll be traveling in Europe, adjust your ATM withdrawal limit if needed, and make sure you know the four-digit PIN for each of your cards, both debit and credit (as you may need to use **chip-and-PIN** for certain purchases). Allow time to receive your PIN by mail.

While most transactions are by card these days, **cash** can help you out of a jam if your card randomly doesn't work, and can be useful to pay for tips and local guides. Wait until you arrive to get euros using your **debit card** (airports have plenty of cash machines). European ATMs accept US debit cards with a Visa or Mastercard logo and work just like they do at home—except they spit out local currency instead of dollars. When possible, withdraw cash from a bank-run ATM located just outside that bank (they usually charge lower fees and are more secure).

Whether withdrawing cash at an ATM or paying with a credit card, you'll often be asked whether you want the transaction processed in dollars or in the local currency. To avoid a poor exchange rate, always refuse the conversion and *choose the local currency*.

Although rare, some US cards may not work at self-service payment machines (such as transit-ticket kiosks, tollbooths, or fuel pumps). Usually a tap-to-pay card does the trick in these situations. Carry cash as a backup and look for a cashier who can process your payment if your card is rejected.

Before you leave home, let your bank know when and where you'll be using your credit and debit cards. To keep your cash, cards, and valuables safe when traveling, wear a **money belt**.

STAYING CONNECTED

The simplest solution is to bring your own device—mobile phone, tablet, or laptop—and use it just as you would at home (following the money-saving tips below). For more on phoning, see RickSteves.com/phoning. For a one-hour talk covering tech issues for travelers, see RickSteves.com/mobile-travel-skills.

To Call from a US Phone: Phone numbers in this book are presented exactly as you would dial them from a US mobile phone. For international access, press and hold the 0 key until you get a + sign, then dial the country code (44 for Northern Ireland) and phone number (omit the initial zero that's used for domestic calls). To dial from a US landline, replace + with 011 (US/Canada international access code).

From a European Landline: Replace + with 00 (Europe international access code), then dial the country code (44 for Northern Ireland) and phone number (omitting the initial zero).

Within Northern Ireland: To place a domestic call (from a Northern Ireland landline or mobile), drop the +44 and dial the phone number (including the initial zero).

Tips: If you bring your mobile phone, consider signing up for an international plan; most providers offer a simple bundle that includes calling, messaging, and data.

Use Wi-Fi whenever possible. Most hotels and many cafés

Sleep Code

Hotels are classified based on the average price of a standard en suite double room with breakfast in high season.

$$$$	**Splurge:** Most rooms over £140
$$$	**Expensive:** £110-140
$$	**Moderate:** £80-110
$	**Budget:** £50-80
¢	**Backpacker:** Under £50
RS%	**Rick Steves discount**

Unless otherwise noted, credit cards are accepted and free Wi-Fi is available. Comparison-shop by checking prices at several hotels (on each hotel's own website, on a booking site, or by email). For the best deal, *book directly with the hotel.* Ask for a discount if paying in cash; if the listing includes **RS%**, request a Rick Steves discount.

---

offer free Wi-Fi, and you may also find it at tourist information offices (TIs), major museums, public-transit hubs, and aboard trains and buses. With Wi-Fi you can use your phone or tablet to make free or low-cost calls via a calling app such as Skype, WhatsApp, FaceTime, and Google Meet. When you need to get online but can't find Wi-Fi, turn on your cellular network (or turn off airplane mode) just long enough for the task at hand.

Most **hotels** charge a fee for placing calls—ask for rates before you dial. You can use a prepaid international phone card (usually available at newsstands, tobacco shops, and train stations) to call out from your hotel.

SLEEPING

I've categorized my recommended accommodations based on price, indicated with a dollar-sign rating (see sidebar). Book your accommodations as soon as your itinerary is set, especially if you want to stay at one of my top listings or if you'll be traveling during busy times.

Once your dates are set, compare prices at several hotels. You can do this by checking hotel websites and booking sites such as Hotels.com or Booking.com. After you've zeroed in on your choice, **book directly with the hotel itself.** This increases the chances that the hotelier will be able to accommodate special needs or requests (such as shifting your reservation). And when you book on the hotel's website, by email, or by phone, the owner avoids the commission paid to booking sites, giving them wiggle room to offer you a discount, a nicer room, or a free breakfast.

For family-run hotels, it's generally best to book your room directly via email or phone. Here's what they'll want to know: number and type of rooms; number of nights; arrival date; depar-

Restaurant Code

Eateries in this book are categorized according to the average cost of a typical main course. Drinks, desserts, and splurge items can raise the price considerably.

$$$$	**Splurge:** Most main courses over £20
$$$	**Pricier:** £15-20
$$	**Moderate:** £10-15
$	**Budget:** Under £10

In Northern Ireland, carryout fish-and-chips and other takeout food is **$**; a basic pub or sit-down eatery is **$$**; a gastropub or casual but more upscale restaurant is **$$$**; and a swanky splurge is **$$$$**.

ture date; any special requests; and applicable discounts (such as a Rick Steves discount, cash discount, or promotional rate). Use the European style for writing dates: day/month/year.

Note that to be called a "hotel" in Ireland, a place must have certain amenities, including a 24-hour reception (though this rule is loosely applied). An "en suite" room has a bathroom (toilet and shower/tub) inside the room; a room with a "private bathroom" can mean that the bathroom is all yours, but it's across the hall.

Some hotels extend a discount to those who pay cash or stay longer than three nights. And some accommodations offer a special discount for Rick Steves readers, indicated in this guidebook by the abbreviation **"RS%."**

Compared to hotels, bed-and-breakfast places give you double the cultural intimacy for half the price. Personal touches, whether it's joining my hosts for afternoon tea or relaxing by a common fireplace at the end of the day, make staying at a B&B my preferred choice. Many B&Bs take credit cards but may add the card service fee to your bill (about 3 percent). If you'll need to pay cash for your room, plan ahead.

A short-term rental—whether an apartment, house, or room in a private residence—is a popular alternative, especially if you plan to settle in one location for several nights. Websites such as Airbnb, FlipKey, Booking.com, and VRBO let you browse a wide range of properties. Alternatively, rental agencies such as InterhomeUSA.com and RentaVilla.com can provide a more personalized service. Northern Ireland's tourism website (www.discovernorthernireland.com) is also a reliable source for rentals.

EATING

I've categorized my recommended eateries based on the average price of a typical main course, indicated with a dollar-sign rating (see sidebar). The traditional "Ulster Fry" breakfast is a hearty way to start the day—with juice, tea or coffee, cereal, eggs, bacon, sausage, toast, a grilled tomato, sautéed mushrooms, and black pudding. Toast is served with butter and marmalade. This meal tides many travelers over until dinner. To dine affordably at classier restaurants, look for "early-bird specials" (sometimes called "pre-theater menus"), which allow you to eat well but early (around 17:30-19:00).

Smart travelers use pubs (short for "public houses") to eat, drink, get out of the rain, and make new friends. Pub grub is Northern Ireland's best eating value (although not every pub serves food). Pubs that are attached to restaurants are more likely to have fresh, made-to-order food. For about $20, you'll get a basic meal in convivial surroundings. The menu is hearty and traditional: stews, soups, fish-and-chips, meat, cabbage, potatoes, and—in coastal areas—fresh seafood such as mackerel, mussels, and Atlantic salmon. Order drinks and meals at the bar, and pay as you order.

Most pubs have lagers (cold, refreshing, American-style beer), ales (amber-colored, cellar-temperature beer), bitters (hop-flavored ale, perhaps the most typical British beer), and stouts (dark and somewhat bitter—the most famous is Guinness, of course).

Tipping: At a sit-down place with table service, tip about 10-12 percent—unless the service charge is already listed on the bill. If you order at a counter, there's no need to tip.

TRANSPORTATION

By Car: It's cheaper to arrange most car rentals from the US. For tips on your insurance options, see RickSteves.com/cdw (if you're also going to the Republic of Ireland, note that many credit-card companies do not offer collision coverage for rentals in the Republic). Bring your driver's license.

A car is an expensive headache in Belfast. But if venturing into the countryside, I enjoy the freedom of a rental car for reaching far-flung rural sights. For navigation, the mapping app on your phone works fine. On an all-Ireland trip, you can drive your rental car from Northern Ireland into the Republic of Ireland, but you will pay a drop-off charge (as much as $200) if you return it across the border from where you rented it.

Some companies in Northern Ireland won't rent to anyone over 69. In the Republic of Ireland, you generally can't rent a car if you're 75 or older, and you'll usually pay extra if you're 70-74. In Northern Ireland, the speed limit is in miles per hour; in the Republic, it's in kilometers per hour.

Remember that people throughout Ireland drive on the left side of the road (and the driver sits on the right side of the car). You'll quickly master the many roundabouts: Traffic moves clockwise, cars inside the roundabout have the right-of-way, and entering traffic yields (look to your right as you merge). Note that road-surveillance cameras strictly enforce speed limits by automatically snapping photos of speeders' license plates, then mailing them a bill.

Local road etiquette is similar to that in the US. Ask your car-rental company for details, or check the US State Department website (www.travel.state.gov, search for your country in the "Learn About Your Destination" box, then select "Travel and Transportation").

By Train and Bus: You can check train and bus schedules at Translink.co.uk. For trains within Northern Ireland, it's standard to buy tickets in stations (or onboard if boarding at a small station that doesn't sell tickets). Most of Translink's online ticket options are for home delivery in Ireland, not electronic. To see if a rail pass could save you money, check RickSteves.com/rail.

Long-distance buses (called "coaches") are about a third slower than trains, but they're also much cheaper. Bus stations are normally at or near train stations. **Translink** serves Northern Ireland (www.translink.co.uk). **Dublin Coach** covers Belfast, Dublin, Ennis, Killarney, Tralee, Kildare, Kilkenny, and Waterford (www.dublincoach.ie, book online at least three hours ahead or pay with credit card onboard).

HELPFUL HINTS

Travel Advisories: Before traveling, check updated health and safety conditions, including restrictions for your destination, on the travel pages of the US State Department (www.travel.state.gov) and Centers for Disease Control and Prevention (www.cdc.gov/travel). The US embassy website for the UK is also a good source of information (see below).

Covid Vaccine/Test Requirements: It's possible you'll need to present proof of vaccination against the coronavirus and/or a negative Covid-19 test result to board a plane to Europe or back to the US. Carefully check requirements for each country you'll visit well before you depart, and again a few days before your trip. See the websites listed above for current requirements.

Emergency and Medical Help: For any emergency service—ambulance, police, or fire—call **112** from a mobile phone or landline. If you get sick, do as the Irish do and go to a pharmacist for advice. Or ask at your hotel for help—they'll know the nearest medical and emergency services.

For **passport problems,** contact the **US Consulate** (in Belfast—by appointment only, dial +44 28 9038 6100, after-hours emergency dial +44 12 5350 1106, http://uk.usembassy.gov/embassy-consulates/belfast). The **Canadian Consulate** in Belfast (+44 28 9754 2405) doesn't offer passport services; instead contact the Canadian High Commission in London (www.unitedking-dom.gc.ca).

ETIAS Registration: The European Union may soon require US and Canadian citizens to register online with the European Travel Information and Authorization System (ETIAS) before entering any Schengen Zone countries (quick and easy process). For the latest, check www.etiasvisa.com.

Theft or Loss: To replace a passport, you'll need to go in person to an embassy or consulate (see above). Cancel and replace your credit and debit cards by calling these 24-hour US numbers: Visa (dial +1 303 967 1096), Mastercard (dial +1 636 722 7111), and American Express (dial +1 336 393 1111). From a landline, you can call these US numbers collect by going through a local operator. File a police report either on the spot or within a day or two; you'll need it to submit an insurance claim for lost or stolen items, and it can help with replacing your passport or credit and debit cards. For more information, see RickSteves.com/help.

Time: Northern Ireland uses the 24-hour clock. It's the same through 12:00 noon, then keep going: 13:00, 14:00, and so on. Ireland, like Great Britain, is five/eight hours ahead of the East/West Coasts of the US (and one hour earlier than most of continental Europe).

Business Hours: In Ireland, most stores are open Monday through Saturday from roughly 10:00 to 17:30 or 18:00, with a late night on Wednesday or Thursday (until 19:00 or 20:00), depending on the neighborhood. On Sundays, sightseeing attractions are generally open (with limited hours), while banks and many shops are closed.

Sightseeing: Many popular sights come with long lines—not to get in, but to buy a ticket. Visitors who buy tickets online in advance (or who have a museum pass covering these key sights) can skip the line and waltz right in. Advance tickets are generally timed-entry, meaning you're guaranteed admission on a certain date and time.

For some sights, buying ahead is required (tickets aren't sold at the sight and it's the only way to get in). At other sights, buying ahead is recommended to skip the line and save time. And for many sights, advance tickets are available but unnecessary: At these uncrowded sights you can simply arrive, buy a ticket, and go in.

Use my advice in this book as a guide. Note any must-see sights that sell out long in advance and be prepared to buy tickets early. If you do your research, you'll know the smart strategy.

Given how precious your vacation time is, I'd book in advance both where it's required (as soon as your dates are firm) and where it will save time in a long line (in some cases, you can do this even

PRACTICALITIES

on the day you plan to visit).

Holidays and Festivals: Northern Ireland celebrates many holidays, which can close sights and attract crowds (book hotel rooms ahead). For information on holidays and festivals, check Northern Ireland's tourism website, DiscoverNorthernIreland.com. For a simple list showing major—though not all—events, see RickSteves.com/festivals.

Numbers and Stumblers: What Americans call the second floor of a building is the first floor in Europe. Europeans write dates as day/month/year, so Christmas 2023 is 25/12/23. For most measurements, Northern Ireland uses the metric system: A kilogram is 2.2 pounds, and a liter is about a quart. For driving distances, they use miles.

RESOURCES FROM RICK STEVES

This Snapshot guide, excerpted from my latest edition of *Rick Steves Ireland,* is one of many titles in my series of guidebooks on European travel. I also produce a public television series, *Rick Steves' Europe,* and a public radio show, *Travel with Rick Steves.* My free online video library, Rick Steves Classroom Europe, offers a searchable database of short video clips on European history, culture, and geography (Classroom.RickSteves.com). My website, RickSteves.com, offers free travel information, a forum for travelers' comments, guidebook updates, my travel blog, an online travel store, and information on European rail passes and our tours of Europe. If you're bringing a mobile device, you can download my free Rick Steves Audio Europe app featuring dozens of self-guided audio tours of the top sights in Europe, and travel interviews about Ireland. For more information, see RickSteves.com/audioeurope. You can also follow me on Facebook, Twitter, and Instagram.

ADDITIONAL RESOURCES

Northern Ireland Tourist Information: www.discovernorthernireland.com
Passports and Red Tape: www.travel.state.gov
Packing List: www.ricksteves.com/packing
Travel Insurance: www.ricksteves.com/insurance
Cheap Flights: www.kayak.com or www.google.com/flights
Airplane Carry-on Restrictions: www.tsa.gov
Updates for This Book: www.ricksteves.com/update

HOW WAS YOUR TRIP?

To share your tips, concerns, and discoveries after using this book, please fill out the survey at RickSteves.com/feedback. Thanks in advance—it helps a lot.

PRACTICALITIES

INDEX

Start your trip at

Our website enhances this book and turns

Explore Europe

At ricksteves.com you can browse through thousands of articles, videos, photos and radio interviews, plus find a wealth of money-saving travel tips for planning your dream trip. And with our mobile-friendly website, you can easily access all this great travel information anywhere you go.

TV Shows

Preview the places you'll visit by watching entire half-hour episodes of *Rick Steves' Europe* (choose from all 100 shows) on-demand, for free.

ricksteves.com

your travel dreams into affordable reality

Radio Interviews

Enjoy ready access to Rick's vast library of radio interviews covering travel tips and cultural insights that relate specifically to your Europe travel plans.

Travel Forums

Learn, ask, share! Our online community of savvy travelers is a great resource for first-time travelers to Europe, as well as seasoned pros.

Travel News

Subscribe to our free Travel News e-newsletter, and get monthly updates from Rick on what's happening in Europe.

Classroom Europe®

Check out our free resource for educators with 500 short video clips from the *Rick Steves' Europe* TV show.

Audio Europe™

Pack Light and Right

Gear up for your next adventure at ricksteves.com

Light Luggage

Pack light and right with Rick Steves' affordable, custom-designed rolling carry-on bags, backpacks, day packs and shoulder bags.

Accessories

From packing cubes to moneybelts and beyond, Rick has personally selected the travel goodies that will help your trip go smoother.

Shop at ricksteves.com

Rick Steves has

Experience maximum Europe

Save time and energy

This guidebook is your independent-travel toolkit. But for all it delivers, it's still up to you to devote the time and energy it takes to manage the preparation and logistics that are essential for a happy trip. If that's a hassle, there's a solution.

Rick Steves Tours

A Rick Steves tour takes you to Europe's most interesting places with great

with minimum stress

guides and small groups. We follow Rick's favorite itineraries, ride in comfy buses, stay in family-run hotels, and bring you intimately close to the Europe you've traveled so far to see. Most importantly, we take away the logistical headaches so you can focus on the fun.

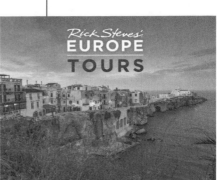

Join the fun

This year we'll take thousands of free-spirited travelers—nearly half of them repeat customers— along with us on 50 different itineraries, from Athens to Istanbul. Is a Rick Steves tour the right fit for your travel dreams?

Find out at ricksteves.com, where you can also check seat availability and sign up. Europe is best experienced with happy travel partners. We hope you can join us.

A Guide for Every Trip

BEST OF GUIDES

Full-color guides in an easy-to-scan format. Focused on top sights and experiences in the most popular European destinations

Best of England
Best of Europe
Best of France
Best of Germany
Best of Ireland
Best of Italy
Best of Scotland
Best of Spain

COMPREHENSIVE GUIDES

City, country, and regional guides printed on Bible-thin paper. Packed with detailed coverage for a multi-week trip exploring iconic sights and venturing off the beaten path

Amsterdam & the Netherlands
Barcelona
Belgium: Bruges, Brussels,
   Antwerp & Ghent
Berlin
Budapest
Croatia & Slovenia
Eastern Europe
England
Florence & Tuscany
France
Germany
Great Britain
Greece: Athens & the Peloponnese
Iceland
Ireland
Istanbul
Italy
London
Paris
Portugal
Prague & the Czech Republic
Provence & the French Riviera
Rome
Scandinavia
Scotland
Sicily
Spain
Switzerland
Venice
Vienna, Salzburg & Tirol

HE BEST OF ROME

e, Italy's capital, is studded with
n remnants and floodlit-fountain
s. From the Vatican to the Colos-
. with crazy traffic in between, Rome
derful, huge, and exhausting. The
, the heat, and the weighty history

of the Eternal City where Caesars walked
can make tourists wilt. Recharge by taking siestas, gelato breaks, and after-dark
walks, strolling from one atmospheric
square to another in the refreshing evening air.

Pantheon—which
domt until the
2,000 years old
over 1,500).

Athens in the *Vat-
s the humanistic

diators fought
other, entertaining

POCKET GUIDES
Compact color guides for shorter trips

Amsterdam	Paris
Athens	Prague
Barcelona	Rome
Florence	Venice
Italy's Cinque Terre	Vienna
London	
Munich & Salzburg	

SNAPSHOT GUIDES
Focused single-destination coverage

Basque Country: Spain & France
Copenhagen & the Best of Denmark
Dublin
Dubrovnik
Edinburgh
Hill Towns of Central Italy
Krakow, Warsaw & Gdansk
Lisbon
Loire Valley
Madrid & Toledo
Milan & the Italian Lakes District
Naples & the Amalfi Coast
Nice & the French Riviera
Normandy
Northern Ireland
Norway
Reykjavík
Rothenburg & the Rhine
Sevilla, Granada & Southern Spain
St. Petersburg, Helsinki & Tallinn
Stockholm

CRUISE PORTS GUIDES
Reference for cruise ports of call

Mediterranean Cruise Ports
Scandinavian & Northern European
  Cruise Ports

Complete your library with...

TRAVEL SKILLS & CULTURE
*Study up on travel skills and gain
insight on history and culture*

Europe 101
Europe Through the Back Door
Europe's Top 100 Masterpieces
European Christmas
European Easter
European Festivals
For the Love of Europe
Italy for Food Lovers
Travel as a Political Act

PHRASE BOOKS & DICTIONARIES
French
French, Italian & German
German
Italian
Portuguese
Spanish

PLANNING MAPS
Britain, Ireland & London
Europe
France & Paris
Germany, Austria & Switzerland
Iceland
Ireland
Italy
Scotland
Spain & Portugal

Photo Credits

Avalon Travel
Hachette Book Group
1700 Fourth Street
Berkeley, CA 94710

Printed in Canada by Friesens.
7th Edition. First printing January 2023.

ISBN 978-1-64171-529-4

For the latest on Rick's talks, guidebooks, tours, public television series, and public radio show, contact Rick Steves' Europe, 130 Fourth Avenue North, Edmonds, WA 98020, +1 425 771 8303, RickSteves.com, rick@ricksteves.com.

Rick Steves' Europe
Managing Editor: Jennifer Madison Davis
Assistant Managing Editor: Cathy Lu
Editors: Glenn Eriksen, Suzanne Kotz, Rosie Leutzinger, Teresa Nemeth, Jessica Shaw, Carrie Shepherd
Editorial & Production Assistant: Megan Simms
Researchers: Ben Curtis, Cathy Lu
Contributor: Gene Openshaw
Graphic Content Director: Sandra Hundacker
Maps & Graphics: Orin Dubrow, David C. Hoerlein, Lauren Mills, Mary Rostad, Laura Terrenzio

Avalon Travel
Senior Editor and Series Manager: Madhu Prasher
Associate Managing Editor: Jamie Andrade
Editor: Rachael Sablik
Proofreader: Patrick Collins
Indexer: Stephen Callahan
Production: Christine DeLorenzo, Lisi Baldwin, Rue Flaherty, Jane Musser, Ravina Schneider
Cover Design: Kimberly Glyder Design
Maps & Graphics: Kat Bennett

Let's Keep on Travelin'

Your trip doesn't need to end.

Follow Rick on social media!